SELECTED DELANTY

Greg Delanty, August 2017, by Anthony Sini

SELECTED DELANTY

Poems and translations by Greg Delanty
chosen and introduced by Archie Burnett

2017
Un-Gyve Press
Boston

Designed by Un-Gyve Limited

Manufactured in the United States of America

FIRST EDITION

10 9 8 7 6 5 4 3 2 1

Library of Congress Control Number:
2017955307

ISBN: 978-0-9993632-1-8

Contents

From *The Greek Anthology, Book XVII* (2012)

Translations of Contemporary Irish Language Poets

Uncollected Poems

BOOKS BY GREG DELANTY

Poetry Collections
Cast in the Fire
Southward
American Wake
The Hellbox
The Blind Stitch
The Ship of Birth
Collected Poems 1986-2006
The New Citizen Army
Loosestrife
The Greek Anthology, Book XVII (retitled *Book Seventeen* in US edition)

Special Poetry Editions
The Fifth Province
Striped Ink

Translations
Selected Poems of Kyriakos Charalambides

Anthologies
Jumping Off Shadows: Selected Contemporary Irish Poets
   (with Nuala Ní Dhomhnaill)
New and Selected Poems of Patrick Galvin
   (with Robert Welch)
The Word Exchange, Anglo-Saxon Poetry in Translation
   (with Michael Matto)
So Little Time: Words and Images for a World in Climate Crisis

A NOTE FROM THE AUTHOR:

The poems here are in their final definitive form. This includes the indentations which have varied in other publications. The indented spaces of my poems not in this volume should be similarly followed.

I always meant "The Splinters" be read as a poem for voices (as with *The Greek Anthology, Book XVII*). The speakers' names in Part III, not part of the poem, should not be spoken. The last two speakers say one poem, the first eight lines by Louis MacNeice, the second by Dylan Thomas. Both visited the area. All the other speakers have an association with the region.

ACKNOWLEDGEMENTS

Poems from the last section first appeared in *Agenda*, *The Irish Times*, *Poetry Review*, *Quarryman*, *So Little Time — Words and Images for a World in Climate Crisis* (Green Writer's Press, 2014) and *Southward*. I would like to thank their editors and the editors of newspapers, journals, magazines and anthologies who first published poems from previous collections, as well as the editors and publishers of those collections, especially Carcanet Press and Louisiana State University Press.

I would particularly like to thank Saint Michael's College, Vermont. The college has supported me now for thirty years, allowing me to pursue much of this work.

It is impossible for me not to acknowledge Christopher Ricks, who has since 1986 looked over and helped me with many of the poems here. I cannot say enough about what he means to me, himself, his help, and his selflessness. My life would have been very different without him, and without him my life and poetry would not have been better.

I am also very grateful to the great Jonathan Williams, the literary agent who is much more than that, and who has been a securing help from the start.

This Sweeney will miss sending this book to Seamus Heaney and getting his welcome and welcoming response, and I will miss being together with him later over a drink to wish the book good fortune. He buoyed up so many of us, made each of us feel that we were worthwhile, that we were adding.

I am also especially indebted to Robert Milkwood Thomas (just in case this book is lucky enough to get to you). You have fortified me daily since I was thirteen, and it was from your work that I first discovered the music and wonder of words, and learned how an artist must change and renew herself or himself as each progresses.

Finally, I want to thank those who helped with the translations, Katharine Washburn (Aristophanes and Euripides), Gail Holst-Warhaft (Kyriakos Charalambides), Michael Matto (Old English) and Liam Ó Muirthile for the Irish language ones. They provided literal cribs and advice. Without them, I could not have done these translations.

There are others to thank, and I will do that personally, when the time comes, but there are some who are now dead, and whom I'd like to acknowledge for their help along the way: Anthony Cronin, John Engels, Galway Kinnell, John Montague, Alastair Reid, John Reiss, and Katharine Washburn.

The following poems were first published in *The Atlantic Monthly*: 'Loosestrife' (November 2005), 'Tagging the Stealer' (June 1997), 'The Compositor' (August 1995) and 'After Viewing *The Bowling Match at Castlemary, Cloyne, 1847*' (February 1995).

'After Viewing *The Bowling Match at Castlemary, Cloyne, 1847*': The date in the title of the painting in the Crawford Municipal Art Gallery has come into question. It is now thought more likely to date to the early 1840s, as a description matching this painting can be found in the *Cork Examiner*, 6th October 1842. It is most likely, therefore, that this was painted in 1841/42, during the time of another famine in which 10% of the population died. In any case, this was painted during a time of famine and exile in Ireland. This poem, with the same title as in this book, was first published along with the painting in *The Atlantic Monthly* (now *The Atlantic*), February 1995.

For more detailed explanations of slang words, please see Terence Patrick Dolan's *A Dictionary of Hiberno-English: The Irish Use of English* (Dublin: Gill & Macmillan, 1999), Bernard Share's *Slanguage — A Dictionary of Irish Slang* (Dublin: Gill & Macmillan, 1997), Seán Beecher's *A Dictionary of Cork Slang* (Cork: Goldy Angel Press, 1983), and the website www.hiberno-english.com.

For *The Hellbox* I consulted Joseph Moxon's *Mechanick Exercises on the Whole Art of Printing* as well as general printing handbooks.

Greg Delanty

BIOGRAPHY

GREG DELANTY was born in Cork City, Ireland, in 1958 and lived in Cork until 1986. He became a US citizen in 1992, and retains his Irish citizenship. He now lives most of the year in Burlington, Vermont, where he is the Poet in Residence at St. Michael's College. He returns to his Irish home in Derrynane, County Kerry, each summer. Delanty has either written or edited seventeen books and has received numerous awards for his poetry including The Patrick Kavanagh Award (1983), The Allan Dowling Poetry Fellowship (1986), the Austin Clarke Centenary Poetry Award (1997), and a Guggenheim Fellowship for poetry (2008). He has received an Irish Arts Council Bursary, and has been widely anthologized.

Greg Delanty's papers up to 2010 are housed in The National Library of Ireland. His papers from 2010 to 2015 are housed in the Boole Library of University College Cork.

He is Past President of The Association of Literary Scholars, Critics, and Writers (ALSCW).

ARCHIE BURNETT is Director of the Editorial Institute and Professor of English at Boston University. He took a first in English at Edinburgh University before doing a DPhil at Oxford on Milton's language. From 1974 to 1978 he was Junior Research Fellow in English at St John's College, Oxford, and subsequently Lecturer and eventually Professor at Oxford Brookes University. His major publications are *Milton's Style: The Shorter Poems, Paradise Regained and Samson Agonistes* (1981), the Oxford editions of *The Poems of A. E. Housman* (1997) and *The Letters of A. E. Housman* (2007), and *Philip Larkin: The Complete Poems* (Faber, 2012). His editorial work has drawn the highest praise. He is currently preparing a multi-volume edition of the collected prose of T. S. Eliot for Faber.

INTRODUCTION

Greg Delanty is Irish-American. Not Irish American, which would imply a bond at once looser and hierarchical (American, but Irish too). And not, unthinkably, 'American-Irish', such is the larger inclusiveness of the United States. From the brief biography that precedes this introduction, it will be clear that he divides himself culturally, and sometimes physically, between Ireland and the United States. He has written poems set in each place and poems that combine the two cultures; but he also writes poems that belong to neither place — visionary poems that transcend locality entirely and embrace larger human concerns.

He has been regarded as both a poet in the Irish tradition and as an American, and specifically Vermont, poet, and as *the* poet who speaks as one of, and for, the Irish-in-America. When Irish slang and other colloquialisms infiltrate the language of the poetry, they keep it from any trace of pomposity ('shebang', 'ballyhoo', 'shenanigans', 'blarneying'), and ground observation with no-nonsense frankness ('Bozo', 'fatso', 'snazzy'). The particular mix of literary and demotic language ('lingo' would be his word) becomes a hallmark:

> Two magpies scuffle, all cacophony.
>
> They vie for a partner who seems coy.
> These stroppy, sozzled graduates in tuxedos
> cop she's long gone with another boy
> and flap off, the best of buddies.
>> 'Two for Joy' p. 14

> Can you still hear a distant train whistle blow?
> Wet my whistle with a slug of Guinness.
> What is the texture of fresh-fallen snow?
>> 'The Splinters' p. 26

> I take the bait and watch floors of laboring women and men flit by,
>   caught in the lift's mesh of Xs,
> drowned out by the machines' hullabaloo.
>> 'Striped Ink' p. 46

We, a bunch of greencard Irish,
    vamp it under the cathedral arches
of Brooklyn Bridge that's strung like a harp.

        'We Will Not Play the Harp Backward Now, No' p. 52

                Nothing done
and it's lunchtime, rushing to a meeting,
held up by white-out traffic, the snow
    calling a halt to the daily life-and-death tedium:
committees, bills, email, post. If we croaked today
    what difference would it make?

                'White Out' p. 181

    And should we each manage to wrestle
our own particular Trauma to the ground and tame him,
    there is Thanatos — his natural father — waiting
at the end of it all, the Bigwig behind all the trouble.

                'Wonder of Wonders' p. 214

The informality can be effective. In 'Two for Joy', for instance —

The shadows of a school of whale-grey clouds,
    sweeping the sea's surface, bamboozle
fish into thinking that leviathans glide
    overhead

— 'bamboozle' is not at all expected alongside the metaphors of clouds
sweeping the sea and leviathans gliding and the precise association of
'school' with 'whale' that sustains the illusion of leviathans overhead. But
the surprise of the word is apt.
    When the language clashes, it can signal a clash of cultures. In 'Elegy
for an Aunt', during a visit to India —

                I lost my way and there
    wasn't a sinner to direct me
in the maze of alleys narrower than the lanes off Cork's
    norrie quays, and as manky,
when around one corner trots a funeral of Hindus
    with fanny-all on but their dhoti baydinahs.

— 'norrie', 'manky' and 'fanny-all on' ground the experience back in
Ireland, while 'dhoti baydinahs', joining the word for a sarong pulled up
between the legs to Cork slang for a swimming costume, acknowledges

difference; but the juxtapositions also catch the comic improbability of the encounter of the two cultures in all its bizarrerie. And yet, a humane cross-cultural connection in language that erodes difference is made too: the Hindu funeral reminds him of a recent funeral back in Ireland:

> I stepped aside from pallbearers shouldering
>   a tinsel-covered body about the size of Kitty's,
> whose bier I bore only weeks ago on the hills
>   down to the ghats
> of chemical factories lining the Lee, our Ganges.

In the same poem, the single word 'dekkoed' (meaning 'saw', 'took a look at') establishes a commonality between peoples: it is in fact a Hindi word that became British Army slang before passing into general usage:

> I doubt I could have gone farther from whatever home is
>   under the embers of the Indian night
> as I dekkoed a mourner scrawl the ash tilak of his dead
>   before he swept the remains into
> the heaven of the Ganges; the wherever of the hereafter.

Linguistically, Delanty often positions himself between or across cultures like this. 'The Yank' is a telling instance. It is addressed *'to the Irish-Irish'*. (Is there any other kind? Yes, Irish-American). The Yank is the poet returning to Ireland, reflecting ruefully that he never thought as an Irish child who once mocked busloads of visiting Yanks

> that I'd one day come back
> a returned Yank myself, and you'd mock me
> when I let slip *restroom* or *gas station*.
> You accuse me of scoffing too many hot dogs,
> siding unwittingly with my Vermont physician.

To 'let slip' American phrases is unwitting too, and betrays American identity; but in this case it also, in a different sense, betrays Irish identity, hence the guilty self-consciousness when the Irish people he knows side with a 'Vermont physician' they don't know:

> Now I'm even considering daily jogs,
> concerned not so much for my unhealthy state,
> but the scales of your eyes reading my weight.

Such self-consciousness would not be possible without a sense of dual identity and divided allegiance.

So, is 'home' Ireland or America? Both? Neither?:

US

The snow cap of Mount Discovery is like a white hanky,
    the knots tied in four corners on the shiny dome
of a bald man at a blistering All-Ireland final.
    No one here knows what hurling is. A game played by the gods
when they deign to come down and enter the human body.
    Ares, that most unpopular of commanders in chief,
even among his ruthless peers, has made this country his own.
    Two fighter jets on display scissor the sky's blue cloth
to shreds. They fly above our house in pastoral Vermont.
    People nearby cheer. We are far from home.

'Us', but United States too. The opening simile, applied to 'Mount Discovery', has Irish roots: no American but an Irish-American would have thought of it. (Similarly, in the opening poem of *American Wake*, an Irish bowler wears 'trousers | as indecently tight as a baseballer's'.) But 'here', in America, the Irish game of 'hurling' is as unknown as the word and its accompanying mythology. Ares, god of war, has not only immigrated and never left again, but has colonized America imperially — has made the country his own in both senses. The destructive fighter jets fly above 'our house in pastoral Vermont', but the speaker is distanced from the cheering patriotic people 'nearby'. 'We', who live in Vermont, are 'far from home' by being far from pastoral Ireland; but perhaps we are, all of us, not in a place that feels like home. Home is not 'here'. Throughout the poetry 'home' proves elusive:

all are exiled, and in search
of a home

'The Splinters' p. 26

unable to shake the sense
that at any moment they could step out of
the film, out of the cinema and swan

about the Grand Parade, O'Connell Street,
or Eyre Square and feel at home again

'Film Directions for the Underworld' p. 74

the right way
being the lost way and the long way round
being the only way home, it being home.

'The Lost Way' p. 48

> I didn't want to feel a foreigner
> in my own, what would you call it, homeland?
>
> 'The Hellbox' p. 54

The words for people who change their country are themselves highlighted as strange, foreign:

> I ate the lotus of emigration,
> never in a decade of Sundays imagining I'd be here
> to stay, wincing at the word *emigrant*
> that, once uttered, seems to filch me of myself
> the way they say a camera steals a soul.
> And there is that stranger word *immigrant*
> that I've become and that my tongue
> that night stuck on, the stammer itself
> intimating the meaning.
>
> 'The Lost Way' p. 48

> Brand us *exiles, emigrants* if you like.
>
> 'To Those Who Stayed' p. 228

For all that, there is an undeniable impulse in the poems to look back to Ireland, to name the old names of the streets and people, to bring to life the colorful detail of domesticity and childhood (see 'The Lost Way', for instance.) But moving to a different country also sharpens perception of the new, and Delanty has proved to be uncommonly alert to the newness. It is partly for this reason that *The Ship of Birth* is an unparalleled collection of poems celebrating the miracle of the birth of a child.

He sees things, and shows them to us, as though for the first time: 'the perpetual shhh | Of the fall with its white finger to its lips'; 'the caret of geese inserting | themselves peacefully on the day', 'singing thrushes perch on electric wires | Like notes upon a stave', 'an F-16 unzips the sky', 'staunch, monkish puffins', 'A tourist frantically waving a bee away | is conducting the climax of a symphony', 'soldiers, | who plug their gas pump salutes | to their foreheads as generals cruise by', 'winter giving itself its own ticker tape parade', 'fireworks doodling the warm night air'. Such images in their first-sight vividness belong to the 'Martian' school of poetry. The poetry constantly surprises and makes new.

It does this not only through arresting individual phrases but through metaphorical transmutations that make larger connections. The collection *The Hellbox*, for instance, derives multiple associations from the trade of printing, his father's trade (the 'hellbox' a box in which broken and worn type is discarded to be melted down and recast). Printing provides constant reminders of human fallibility:

And the umpteen ways things can foul up
are beyond telling.

'The Composing Room' p. 40

Which in turn causes the poet to reflect on his own acts of composition:

And even if I foul up and the stewards
are right to set *Kill* on my last page and my words

are distributed and thrown in the hellbox,
the real achievement will be that I tried to set
the words right; that I did it with much labor
and not without a font of love.

'The Composing Room' p. 40

The dark source of poetic invention is identified by 'thinking along the lines' of print:

Lately I've been thinking along the lines
of how certain compositors set words out of
their own ink-black darkness —
                        and no matter
how strong the white spirits, they cannot
wash the ink from their hands, stained
like a weeping woman's mascara-smudged face,
or the finger-printed hands of a gangster.

'White Spirits' p. 45

And the print shop and its hellbox are transformed into America, where new lives are made:

                        forecasting how you
and all you composed in your time would be
    dismantled and distributed in the composing room
of America before being finally cast aside,
    melted down and recast in the likes of us,
each life set in its unique and sometimes fitting
    fonts and distributed or flung in
the hellbox, turning up again diffused in others.

'Ligature' p. 47

In his later poetry Delanty has developed and made explicit a new synthesis that recognizes an even greater inter-connectedness. The world is where 'Everything's in touch with everything else' ('Resort'), where 'Nothing exists | without another', where everything is 'made out of nothing rather | than nothing made out of everything' ('Good Company'), where 'To go unnoticed is good' ('Dropping Names') and 'We survive best | in the shadows' ('Understory'); and where even his own mother and father, commemorated in many poems with aching tenderness, are 'mysterious as the night sky, the god | hidden within the dark of the forbidden inner temple' ('Parents'). In 'Wish You Were Here' he thinks of human beings as 'tourists visiting our planet, | circling our heavenly star', and, similarly, in 'The Traveller's Grace', he remarks 'How abnormal to think it normal to find ourselves | on a spinning ball reeling around a star | at thousands of miles per hour from who knows where | to who knows where.'

It is a world where place matters little, where emigration and exile are human spiritual conditions — not at all bound by nationality and not even a fusion of the old and the new. 'To Those Who Stayed' is addressed to people who may feel superior to those who emigrated, but it reminds them that death and change where they have continued to live are altering everything inexorably, 'leaving you nothing and no one, an immigrant | in your own place, the oblivious emigrant.' (Earlier, in 'The Hellbox', he had reflected that his 'home city, emigrating from itself, changed | so hell for leather . . . that some of us felt oddly abandoned'.) 'Trailer' begins with a surprising blend of images from the present and a specific Irish past:

> Something about the quality of sea swaying in the bay at Hydra
> calls to mind the crowd in the Savoy cinema long ago,
> swaying in unison as everyone sang along with the organ-player

But the organ-player's name is forgotten, the 'singsongs' belong to a 'lost world' that's 'gone the way | of cold type, horse troughs, a particular texture of bread, | certain words'. The closing transcendent image of the poem — 'right now everyone's swaying side | to side, a great moving sea in an antique land' — is at once free of location, desolate ('antique land' calling up the bleak vision of the traveler from an 'antique land' in Shelley's 'Ozymandias'), and rapturous. When the poet finds home, and finds himself, in 'The Skunk Moths', it is neither in Ireland nor in America but in a tender vision of the fragile natural world:

> Imagine the Luna's gossamer tulle wings, the tippets
> brushing us, fanning us tenderly, wrapping us in a veil,
> bringing us gently to our knees in a gathering humility,
> brushing aside our mortification, finally at home, natural
> in the natural world — their wings our cocoon — becoming
> ourselves, pinioned resplendence, at last the human mothfly.

Beyond Irish culture and its clashes or fusions with other cultures there is a larger awareness of the natural world and of human life within it. This is what has always underpinned Delanty's politics and his sense of the need to preserve the environment against human ravages. His love of nature is unmistakable (his knowledge of birds being particularly impressive), and it brings with it a responsibility to respect it and protect it. A sense of potential tragedy lies just under many of the poems, but they emerge humanely on the side of decency and hope.

In making this selection I have tried to represent several of his themes and concerns. I have also interspersed among his own poems some of his translations, which show a kindred spirit. Throughout the selection the reader will find a poet who is a tireless experimenter, complex but still accessible, and — none the worse for it — difficult to categorize. In a letter he wrote when he received his copy of *The Greek Anthology, Book XVII* Seamus Heaney paid pertinent tribute to the plenitude that is in the poems:

> The book has freed and founded you at once — it gets in all
> your voices, the extent of your knowledge, the intensity of your
> commitments, the delight of your scepticism, the weight, as
> Shoneen Keogh would say, of your passion, your rage for justice,
> your gumption and humour, your stylistic agility.

It is my hope that the reader of this selection will delight in and come to respect this irrepressible and multifaceted talent, and want to explore further.

He is a poet who is continually revising his poems. I have printed the latest revised versions, some of which have been prepared for this volume. At the end are some poems that are previously unpublished or uncollected.

Archie Burnett
The Editorial Institute
Boston University

From *Cast in the Fire* (1986)

OUT OF THE ORDINARY

Skin-head pigeons strut in a gang
along the road's white line and fly
from under a fuming police car.
Lazy, contented seagulls catch rides
on the conveyor belt of a river —
others glide and hover in the slow air
of a busking tin whistle player
as if conjured from his upside-down hat.
Singing thrushes play on the fret board
of electric wires and a sparrow
arrows upward, seemingly desperate
to enter heaven, not noticing heaven
has descended to the ordinary
as we saunter along Union Quay.

TIE

Without asking, you borrowed your father's black tie,
sure that he had another black tie to wear
should some acquaintance or relation die.
But had he? He should be here somewhere.
But where? Could he be at home on this dark day,
ransacking drawer after drawer for a funeral tie?
Yes, that must be what has kept him away.
Though you are sure you saw him, tieless,
smiling over at you, before you lost him again
among the keening cortege. Leaving you clueless
to his whereabouts, till earth, splattering a coffin
(or was it the wind ululating in each prayer?),
informed you that you can never give your father
back his black tie, though you'll find him everywhere.

INTERROGATIVE

Even the flimsiest, most vulnerable creatures
are equipped with devices to outwit death:
the night moth blends into its surroundings,
lichen-colored, it conceals itself on bark;
other creatures don the colors of a wasp,
fooling predators into believing they can sting;
but how could your father outwit death's grasp,
snatched for ever and too soon, under its dark wing,
always out in the open without sting or cunning?

LEAVETAKING

After you board the train, you sit and wait,
    to begin your first real journey alone.
You read to avoid the window's awkwardness,
    knowing he's anxious to catch your eye,
      loitering out in never-ending rain,
to wave, a bit shy, another final goodbye;
you are afraid of having to wave too soon.

And for the moment you think it's the train
    next to you has begun, but it is yours,
and your face, pressed to the windowpane,
    is distorted and numbed by the icy glass,
      pinning your eyes upon your father
as he cranes to defy your disappearing train.
Both of you waving, eternally, to each other.

FAMILY

to Dermot

Yes, I know your parents hurt you too,
though the neighbors, of course, never knew.
Those times they fought regardless of you,
hearing them declare they rue the day
they met, and compare themselves
to the neighbors, Mr and Mrs Donoghue,
— who were probably arguing next door too —
as dinners went half-eaten and the radio
blasted songs of eternal love without woe,
before a door slammed the house into a no man's
land of tight silence, with you the go-between
and shell-shocked victim of the two;
though the neighbors, of course, never knew.
Yes, I know your parents hurt you too.

From *Southward* (1992)

THE MASTER PRINTER

Though it's May it is the first spring day.
You are giving me a crossbar to school.
I wonder will Adolina Davy or Lily Walsh
notice me in my first long pants.
We weave through fuming, hooting cars,
elated we've outwitted lunchtime traffic.
Our new front wheel is answering the sun.

You inquire am I okay as I wriggle.
I confide it's just my behind is a bit sore.
You laugh, say we haven't far to go.
But I never want to get there.
We wave each other off and I run pell-mell
to buy a pennyworth of Bull's Eyes,
escaping the thought of the line-up bell.

I hide the sweets beneath my inkwell,
but my nothing-to-hide look reveals them
to the all-seeing eyes of Brother Dermot.
He smiles, ordering me to put out one hand
and then the other, caning until
both palms are stinging pulps,
as he has beaten so many, so often,

distorting each palm's destiny.
Did that brother harm you too
by continually summoning you in
to declare that I, your son, was a *bit* slow?
He did not know, blind behind a righteous frown,
that you had the master printer's skill
of being able to read backwards and upside down.

THE EMIGRANT'S APOLOGY
to my mother

As you led us single-file up the main aisle
I prayed you wouldn't pick a front pew,
aware you wanted to be as close as possible
to God and show off your latest hat too.
It wasn't just that I didn't want people
thinking I was religious, but that I knew
my devotion would be threatened by a conspiracy
of giggles no later than the sermon,
unable to take any sort of solemnity.
My strategy once I felt them coming on
was to conjure horrors: homework I had to do
but couldn't, a toothache, a spoon of medicine.
Now all I would have to think of is you
wearing a black scarf alone in a front pew.

BELOW THE DEVIL'S PUNCHBOWL

By the waterfall you knelt
as if in supplication, bathing
your hands and face before drinking.

Unsettled later when informed by a local
that the devil drinks
from the same waters upstream;

recalling the fear, a rush
as well, after drinking from the source
of each babbling poem you write;

yet you ignore the perpetual shhh
of the fall with its white finger to its lips.

TWO FOR JOY

During the night a heavy fall of rain
cleared the air. We can breathe once more.
The sun cools itself on the ocean
that lackadaisically defines the shore.

The shadows of a school of whale-grey clouds,
sweeping the sea's surface, bamboozle
fish into thinking that leviathans glide
overhead and send petrified shoals

ducking for cover in every direction.
The giants beach themselves on Eagle Hill.
Cormorants perch on the rock of Carrigbreakan
with open wings welcoming the drying wind.

Two white butterflies use it
to raddle through the air before they land
for fueling on nodding Forget-Me-Not,
balming out on a heart-shaped leaf.

I wish I could tell them they've no need
to brandish false eyes to scare me off
and maybe somehow they understand
since they close them and *céilí* toward me.

A tourist frantically waving a bee away
is conducting the climax of a symphony.
Another wants to snapshot the soul of the bay.
Two magpies scuffle, all cacophony.

They vie for a partner who seems coy.
These stroppy, sozzled graduates in tuxedos
cop she's long gone with another boy
and flap off, the best of buddies.

A WAKE ON LAKE CHAMPLAIN

As an F-16 unzips the sky
a white-sailed yacht races in
like a surrendering rider
from the plains of the lake, and a boy
conjures doves with a piece of cake.

Gas pumps plug their fingers in their ears.
You can hardly hear a child start to cry.
Her father fails to rock her still.
Afterwards he remarks this jet is guarding
Plattsburgh Nuclear Base or on border drill.

Now she's mesmerized by a duck and drake
teaching paddling, oblivious fledgling
how to play follow-the-leader.
A peace sign spreads in their wake.

From *American Wake* (1995)

AFTER VIEWING *THE BOWLING MATCH AT CASTLEMARY, CLOYNE 1847*

I promised to show you the bowlers
   out the Blarney Road after Sunday mass,
you were so taken with that painting
   of the snazzy, top-hatted peasant class
     all agog at the bowler in full swing,
     down to his open shirt, in trousers
as indecently tight as a baseballer's.

You would relish each fling's span
   along blackberry boreens, and delight
in a dinger of a curve throw
   as the bowl hurls out of sight,
     not to mention the earthy lingo
     and antics of gambling fans,
giving players thumbs-up or down the banks.

It's not just to witness such shenanigans
   for themselves, but to be relieved
from whatever lurks in our background,
   just as the picture's crowd is freed
     of famine and exile darkening the land,
     waiting to see where the bowl spins
off, a planet out of orbit, and who wins.

THE HERITAGE CENTRE, COBH 1993
to Catherine Coakley and Thomas McCarthy

The train might be a time machine
transporting us from a smog-shrouded city.
Chemical plants slouch down
to the Lee, flick past into the future.
We enter the simulated coffin ship,
peruse dioramas of papier-mâché emigrants
poised in various stages of travail,
accompanied by the canned clamor
of goodbyes, hooters, sailors rigging mast.
We are back doing Lent's Stations
from convict ship to the grand finale
of the *Lusitania* and *Titanic*, buried
in the ocean's unopened sepulcher.
The *Titanic*'s washed-up spyglass
is too rusted to extend any further.
Turned the wrong way around,
everything diminishes, goes far off
just as our own island goes further
from what we hope each day. I refrain
from doom-saying theatrics, afraid
I'll sound like that filming diver down
the first captured time in the *Titanic*,
dramatizing the merest chink at every stage,
from first-class cabins, below to the dark,
fathomless eternity of the gashed steerage.

THE YANK
to the Irish-Irish

How were any of us wiseguy kids to know
when we mocked busloads of rotund Yanks
bleating wow along every hedgerow
from Malin Head down to the Lee banks,
searching for the needle in the haystack
of ancestors with names like Muh-hone-ey
or Don-a-hue,
                   that I'd one day come back,
a returned Yank myself, and you'd mock me
when I let slip *restroom* or *gas station*.
You accuse me of scoffing too many hot dogs,
siding unwittingly with my Vermont physician.
Now I'm even considering daily jogs,
concerned not so much for my unhealthy state,
but the scales of your eyes reading my weight.

IN THE LAND OF THE EAGLE

Our first night here we pubcrawled
the Bronx, still too new
for us not to be enthralled
by the street life and brew

of all-night watering holes
with names like *The Shamrock*
or *Galway Shawl*, full of legals
and illegals longing to go back,

lowering pint after pint
of their staggering Irishness,
sláinte-ing the Dubs' winning point,
cursing American Guinness.

After that country for old men
abandoned them like the gannet
abandons its fledgling,
not all of them make it.

Those that do are more
like the wren who flew high
off the eagle of folklore,
prevailing in the contentious sky.

BACKFIRE

You recall how fireworks were invented
to ward off evil, as they rise
above the Milky Way of Manhattan.

They form into blue, red and white stars
floating in brief constellations,
then scatter like blown dandelions.

Loudspeakers welcome back soldiers
who plug their gas pump salutes
to their foreheads as generals cruise by.

Victory dismisses all who died.
Fireworks turn into flares for help
among the bustle and boom of bombardment.

One blossoms into a weeping willow and hangs
above skyscrapers rising like tombstones.

ON THE MARRIAGE OF FRIENDS

So you have chosen the way of the swan;
the way, perhaps, that is not natural
to everyone, but I will not harp on
about heron, bluebird or dotterel,

nor how the male flycatcher pairs
with two females, keeping a mile between,
so neither twigs how the other shares
the same philandering gentleman.

Did you know the life-coupling way
of the swan is also that of the crow?
And there'll be crow-black days
you'll caw at each other with blind gusto.

At other times you will sing
the duet of the black-collared barbet,
with the first part of the song sung
by one and the second by the mate.

We wish you now many such duet days
and sing for you like the red-eyed vireo
who sings nonstop through the summer blaze
on this day you take the way of swan and crow.

THE SHRINKING WORLD
to Mary and Niall on Catherine's first summer

Reading how the European long-tailed tit
builds a perfect domed nest, gathering lichen
for camouflage, feathers to line it
and cobwebs as binding so the nest can

stretch while chicks grow, I thought of you
rushing to crying Catherine, as if her mouth shone
like a finchling's guiding parents through
darkness. If only chainsaw-armed men,

felling whole forests by the minute,
could see you hover around your fledgling,
they would have immediately cut
engines and listened to your lullabying.

But their lumbering motors drone on
in the distance and perhaps approach us.
And what about all those other Catherines,
imperial woodpeckers and birds of paradise?

I sing now like the North American brown thrasher,
who at one point in its song orchestrates
four different notes: one grieves, another
frets, a third prays, but a fourth celebrates.

From THE SPLINTERS

(Skellig Michael) does not belong to any world that you and I have lived and worked in: it is part of our dream world ... then (heading back) we were pursued by terrors, ghosts from Michael....

George Bernard Shaw

I

The ferry furrows
the foam,
leaving a wake
that quickly settles
and forgets us,
as it has forgotten
all those
who've opened these waters:
fisherman, monk, pilgrim and pagan,
some foundering here.
Our mainland
world diminishes.
There is respite.
A cloud engulfs us
out of nowhere
as if the miraculous
were about to appear.
The veil lifts
to reveal the small Skellig
and Skellig Michael
rising like chapel and cathedral.

II

We forget speech, hypnotized by the climb,
concentrating on narrow, rock-hewn steps
that spiral up like the gyres
of the Book of Kells, whirling in labyrinths
of knowledge, turmoil and eternity.
They lead to the beehive huts and oratories
packed with a congregation of sightseers
who whisper in disbelief and reverence
at how those sometime monks lived
in this wind-tugged cloister of shells.

We browse in each dome's live absence
and picnic above the graveyard
that's no bigger than a currach
with a crucifix for helmsman
navigating his crew to the island of the dead.
We're eyed by the staunch, monkish puffins.
Our tongues loosen, but, in keeping
with the somberness of this sun-haloed place,
we chat about the world with an earnestness
that would embarrass us on the mainland.

You tell of medieval monks charting world maps
with countries drawn as humans gorging upon
each other's entangled bodies. We go on to
the lands and demons of the world of poetry.
I'm flummoxed when you ask what poetry is.
I recall how the earliest musical instruments
were hewn out of bones, and that poets
carve their words out of those gone before.
They are the primitive musicians who beat
and blow words back to life. More than that I don't know.

III

[...]

That dusk at Dún an Óir we slaughtered even
the pregnant, whimpering women methodically
while a bloodstained sun drowned in the ocean.
Each fetus struggled in the belly
of each slain mother as desperately
as a lobster dropped in a boiling pot.
Had shed blood been ink, I could still be
quilling *The Faerie Queene*, but I did not
allow a drop to blot a mere sonnet
that you, trapped in complicity, can never
quite break free of. Admit it, hypocrite!
In your time few are not guilty of slaughter.
Even the page you'll pen this upon is of pine
that Amazonians were shot for. I could go on.

(Edmund Spenser)

I lifted the pitch of my grief
    above the storm-lashing waves
for my world breaking on the reefs
    of foreign, land-grabbing knaves,

who ignore dependence upon
    the lowliest plants and creatures
as the hermit crab and cloak anemone
    depend on one another.

But no matter what, you must
    keen for the world's theft
as I keened mine, despite knowing
    soon no one may be left.

(Aodhagán Ó Rathaille)

Lend an ear to one of your own kind
    and do not let yourself be caught
by the winds of lust, like Dante's starlings
    blown this way and that by every gust.

I myself was borne on this wind
    as I rode across country,
always wary that around the next bend
    my life would catch up with me.

My rakish ways squandered energy
    that I should have instilled in song,
more worthy of the muse-gift given to me
    than my odd aisling.

Pay particular heed to me, especially
    since your word-talent is less than mine.
I'm still too bushed to eke out a last line.

(Eoghan Rua Ó Súilleabháin)

Sing up front,
cold-shouldering
the fashionable
low key of your time,
closed, cautious and crabbit
as a farmer.

Sing as open-throated
as my curlew keen.
I supped the red wine
of Art's blood
as he lay slain,
already becoming Cork mud.

Sing as full-throated
as my unmatched plaint;
matching my words
to his cold body
that would never again
rouse to my touch.
My hands wept
that day's icy rain
as I swore to undo
that kowtowing
dribble of a man
who slew my Art
of the winged white horse.

The spirit of that mare
I rode fleeter than any hare,
fleeter than any deer,
fleeter than the wind
through Munster's open country.

Sing your provenance,
our elder province.

(Eibhlín Dubh Ní Chonaill)

I sang not for my own or for beauty's sake
as much as to keep our spirits fired,
knowing as long as we sang we'd not break,
refusing to allow the country be shired.
But it was too much when even our lands
turned hostile and drove us like lapwings
in hard winter, together in dying bands,
our swollen bellies pregnant with nothing.
Even the birds seemed to give up singing.
So I lay down and relinquished song.
But I should have kept up my *amhrán*-ing,
adapting and transmuting their tongue.
Transform the spirit of where you belong,
make something right out of what's wrong.

(Tomás Rua Ó Súilleabháin)

Tell of those weather-sketched
    Attic islanders
who half-tamed their school
    of rocky Blaskets,
water spouting from the blowholes
    of cliffs.

Tell how they were forced
    from their Ithaca,
still dreaming in the surf-rush
    of Irish,
the inland longing for the lilt
    of the sea.

In them uncover the destiny
    of everyone,
for all are exiled and in search
    of a home,
as you settle the eroding
    island of each poem.

(Robin Flower)

[...]

The islands' standing army
of gannets fiercely snap,
stab and peck one another.
Few could match
the spite I unleashed
on any who encroached
into my territory. I spat
with petrel accuracy.
I should have had the wisdom
of the sad-eyed puffins
who let everyone come close,
sensing few mean hurt,
though when forced to tussle
they'll show their worth.
So learn from me.
When I come to mind
don't recall how, feisty,
I knocked nests of words
over the edge,
splattering on the rocks
to the crude squawks of other
ravaging, wing-elbowing birds;
rather think of the winged poems
I hatched, seen,
regardless of time and place,
gliding and gyring
with their own grace.

(Patrick Kavanagh)

Life when it is gone is like a woman
you were glad to be quit of only to find
yourself years later longing for her,
catching her scent on a crowded street.
Tell us of the seagull plundering your picnic
before it wakes you. Tell us of the rain
tapping a pane while you're ensconced
by the fire cradling a pregnant brandy glass.

(Louis MacNeice)

Can you still hear a distant train whistle blow?
Wet my whistle with a slug of Guinness.
What is the texture of fresh-fallen snow?
Do girls still wear their hair in braid?
What's tea? What's the smell of the sea?
Tell me. Tell me. I am beginning to fade.

(Dylan Thomas)

IV

The alarming, silhouetted bird
has a preternatural quality
as it flutters about
my head, drawing me
from sleep's underworld.
I resist its pull.
Everything turns
into dream's usual montage.
Another figure emerges
but says nothing,
as if that's what he came to say.
His face merges into
one of a gagged female.
She shimmers and vanishes.
Dolphins break
beyond Blind Man's Cove,
returning the dead
to Bull Island, transmitting
their encrypted, underwater Morse.
The savant local ferryman
informs us that Skellig Michael
was once a druidic site.
His oil-wrinkled hands tug
the engine cord,
coaxing our boat
out of the cliff-shaded cove.
We withdraw
into the distance,
leaving a disgruntling sense
that we've only touched the tip
of these dark icebergs.

THE CHILDREN OF LIR

Today snow falls in swan-downy flakes
    reminding me of the Children of Lir,
    not solely of Fionnuala and her brothers,
    but all exiles over all the years
with only dolorous songs for company.
    The last note of their singing
    now fills the air — it is the silence
    of snow slowly falling.

From *The Hellbox* (1998)

THE COMPOSITOR

Perhaps it's the smell of printing ink
sets me off out of memory's jumbled font
or maybe it's the printer's lingo
as he relates how phrases came about.

How for instance: *mind your p's and q's*
has as much to do with pints and quarts
and the printer's renown for drink
as it has with those descenders.

But I don't say anything about
how I discovered where *widows* and *orphans*
and *out of sorts* came from the day my father
unnoticed and unexpectedly set *30*

on the bottom of his compositor's page
and left me mystified about the origins
of that end, how to measure a line gauge
and how, since he was first to go,

he slowly and without a word
turned from himself into everyone,
as we turn into that last zero
before finally passing on to the stoneman.

THE CURE

to my father

I drop into the printers and graft
to you with my hangover on hearing
the tall drinking tales of your craft
from an apprentice of yours, latching

on to the old typesetter days like myself.
He swore he could write a book.
I thought of how you were partial yourself
to a jorum or two, but you would look

down on my pint-swaggering and remind me
you kept your drinking to Saturday night,
barring births, weddings, deaths, and maybe
the odd quick one if the company was right.

And for the most part I keep to that too,
but last night was a night I broke
and went on the rantan from bar to
bar, jawing with whichever bloke,

solving the world's problems drink
by drink, cigarette by cigarette, swigging
and puffing away the whole lousy stink.
You nagged away in my head about smoking

and how the butts did away with you.
But I swear the way I stood there
and yakkety-yakked, slagged and blew
smoke into the smoke-shrouded air,

coughing your smoker's cough,
I thought that you had turned into me
or I into you. I laughed your laugh
and then, knowing how you loved company,

I refused to quit the bar and leave you alone
or leave myself alone or whoever we were.
I raised my glass to your surprise return.
Now I hear you guffaw once more

as your apprentice continues to recount
printers' drink lore and asks if I know
comps at Signature O got a complimentary pint.
I joust our way out the door repeating O O O.

THE COMPOSING ROOM

I still see those men haphazardly standing
around the comps' floor, mostly silent,
lost in their latest urgent jobs,
looking up and down as if nodding yes

from what they call their composers' sticks
as they set inverse words and lines
of each page that could be taken for
Greek scripture, declaring:

In the beginning was the Word and the Word
was made cold type and the Word was
coldness, darkness, shiny greyness
and light — and the Word dwelt amongst us.

                            *

Oh, I know these men would laugh this off.
They'd say, if they simply didn't throw
their eyes to heaven, that they were just ordinary
characters trying to keep the devil from the door,

and with luck have enough left over each week
to back a few nags, and go for a few jars.
But they can't say anything or set anything now.
They are scattered from that place that's not

the same any more and many have left
any place we know of in this life,
calling to mind the old names for printing:
The Mysterious Craft or simply *The Mystery*.

I set them up in another city, another country
that's as far away in distance
from that city as it's far in time.
But they are still composing,

cracking the odd joke above
their sticks and galleys on some floor
of some building that is eternally busy
inside me even when I've forgotten

that I've forgotten them; forgetting
the world behind the word —
every time I read the word *world* I wonder
is it a typo and should I delete the *l*.

*

Now again I hanker to know the quality
of each letter: the weight, the texture, the smell,
the shiny new type, the ink-dark shades of old,
the different types of type, the various sizes

within the same font, the measures in ems,
picas, points and units. I'd set the words up,
making something out of all this
that stays standing — all set as masterly

as the words those men set that reveal
something of the mystery behind
and within these letters and the wonder and
the darkness, but with the lightest touch.

*

And the umpteen ways things can foul up
are beyond telling. Maybe the type is off,
or the typesetter may not be up
to the work, if only out of a hangover

setting an *!* where there should be a *?*
or a *b* where there should be a *d*,
or miss aspace or a line or dingbat.
And the proofreaders don't catch the error,

passing the copy on as clean, or the make-up man
fouls the assembly page, or the stoneman errs
as he fastens the page of cold type and furniture
with the chase, turning the quoin's key.

*

Not to speak of the evil eye cast by
fellow composers ready
to knock the words of others, or the bosses
writing on the composition: *Kill.*

Old Shades, keep my words from such eyes
and fretting about that pied world and let me go
on regardless. And even if I foul up and the stewards
are right to set *Kill* on my last page and my words

are distributed and thrown in the hellbox,
the real achievement will be that I tried to set
the words right; that I did it with much labor
and not without a font of love. But that said,

42

*

grant me the skill to free the leaden words
from the words I set, undo their awkwardness,
the weight of each letter of each word
so that the words disappear, fall away

or are forgotten and what remains is the metal
of feeling and thought behind
and beyond the cast of words
dissolving in their own ink wash.

Within this solution we find ourselves,
meeting only here, through *The Mystery*,
but relieved nonetheless to meet, if only
behind the characters of one fly-boy's words.

MODERN TIMES
for Seán Dunne

I've a notion, instead of entering the hereafter
or turning into some mythical tree,
the spirits of dead Shakers enter
the wood they fashioned with such severity.

The frigid, upright, spiny furniture
seems to withdraw as we intrude on each room
set so sparsely in this New Hampshire
ghost town that I can't imagine calling home.

And coming on the antique printer's shop,
with galley pages of *The Shaker Manifesto*
locked by the quoins so no character could drop,
I long for the security of such words.

But I've lost my quoin's key
and all my shaken words fall uneven.

WHITE SPIRITS

In the beginning, typography was denounced
as the Black Art. Though why or by whom
I can't exactly say.
                Perhaps it had to do
with an invention's magic air, or the fear
that the spread of the word would undo souls —
it probably simply came down to printers
being eternally bedaubed in black ink.

Lately I've been thinking along the lines
of how certain compositors set words out of
their own ink-black darkness —
                       and no matter
how strong the white spirits, they cannot
wash the ink from their hands, stained
like a weeping woman's mascara-smudged face,
or the finger-printed hands of a gangster.

STRIPED INK

I'm smack-dab in the old tabula rasa days, bamboozled by the books
adults bow over, musing if their eyes light upon the white or black
    spaces.

*

A boyhood later, still wren-small, on the top storey
   of the Eagle Printing Company,
I see books pour out and believe that if I fish in them
I'll catch the salmon of knowledge, tall-taled to us at school,
out of the river of words, and like Fionn I'll taste
my burning hand and abracadabra I'll fathom what's below the surface.

*

But if I'm burnt, it's later that day, on my first day as pageboy, spaced
   from fixing leads.
The devils Fred and Dommy, typesetting a new book, dispatch me
down to Christy Coughlan on the box floor for a tin of striped ink.
I take the bait and watch floors of laboring women and men flit by,
   caught in the lift's mesh of Xs,
drowned out by the machines' hullabaloo. Somehow, between floors,
   the elevator conks out,
the warning light winking, and I'm stuck on my message and still have
   no inkling.

LIGATURE

This latent mine — these unlaunch'd voices — passionate powers,
Wrath, argument, or praise, or comic leer, or prayer devout,
(Not nonpareil, brevier, bourgeois, long primer merely,)
These ocean waves arousable to fury and to death,
Or sooth'd to ease and sheeny sun and sleep,
Within the pallid slivers slumbering.

                                   Walt Whitman, 'A Font of Type'

I trekked to the Eagle and the unassuming redbrick
   where you first set *Leaves*, forecasting how you
and all you composed in your time would be
   dismantled, distributed in the composing room
of America before being finally cast aside,
   melted down and recast in the likes of us,
each life set in its unique and sometimes fitting
   fonts and distributed or flung in
the hellbox, turning up again diffused in others.
   But it's our time to set our own lives down,
to select and fix them with our own measure
   in a ligature affixing characters who've gone
before to those close by now and way off in the future

THE LOST WAY
to Robert Welch

Snow was general all over Amerikay
as we Kerouaced back from Montreal
trailing our myopic headlights,
nosing through dervishing white smoke.

Miles back we took the wrong turn,
led astray by the Québecois
squabbling in their strange French at the gas station
about which way we should take.
But to give the Canucks the benefit of the doubt,
we may well have got it wrong ourselves,
given how we got lost so often that day, a parody
of Brendan or Odysseus and their mutinous crews.

*

In our rent-a-car Chevrolet Troubadour
I *seanchaí*-ed how I ate the lotus of emigration,
never in a decade of Sundays imagining I'd be here
to stay, wincing at the word *emigrant*
that, once uttered, seems to filch me of myself
the way they say a camera steals a soul.
And there is that stranger word *immigrant*
that I've become and that my tongue
that night stuck on, the stammer itself
intimating the meaning.
                              You remarked,
freeing my tongue's needle
stuck on its damaged record,
how *cúpla dán* of mine are hearkening back,
a kind of grappling for the life buoy's O
of the roads, streets and life of the drowned city
we both hail from. Outsiders,
especially dose from da Pale look down
dare snotty proboscises on our corker Corkonian
dat's not just da closest ding in English to Irish,
but as nare to Elizabedan English *freisin*
— which is as good an excuse as anything for me sonnets —
what wit our *ye* and say how we turn the word beer
into what all went down to da woods. But why *like*
is dropped into every sentence when dare's nuting
to liken the like to — ya know, like — we can't say.

48

As the windshield wipers said no to the snow
we recalled how we labored on dismal, Pre-Vatican II
Latin, Lenten nights to the men's mission, hardly out
of short pants. A partnership of visiting padres
worked on us like a pair of interrogating New York vice,
that must be, since so many of New York's finest are Micks,
where the cops learned questioning techniques.
One spotted guilt in black spots on our tongues,
condemning us to Life in Hell's Alcatraz,
setting us up for his partner
who lured us with immunity, rewards and new identities.

Then there was the hot-footed fretting along Curragh Road,
past Kiely's where we lamped the skimpy bikinied cover girl
of *Titbits* as soon as Mrs Kiely's back was turned,
and where we got the *Victor* and *Hotspur* —
I think on Fridays — after our dads doled out
our weekly pocket money of an English or Irish
threepenny bit. Which was which I could never tell.
I can still recall the forking-out, print-inked hands
of my father, setting gentle words in me, his impress,
and me swearing I'd set words like him some day.

We'd bribe cogs on undone homework mornings
with the currency of Trigger Bars, lucky bags, gobstoppers,
acid drops, Hadji Beys, donkey's grudge, Taytos,
Flakes, Thompson's custard slices, licorice snakes
black as the tongues of our souls . . .
Though I suspect you, being brighter than *mise*, gave cogs,
and for nought, as is your nature. But how could we
out-smart-aleck the holy terrors of our childhoods?:
Sister Benedict, Brother Dermot, Dantro, Leo . . . all
all too ready to root out the dodos, *amadáns*,
goms, slow ones, with endless spelling tests
and the *tuisceal ginideach* of Irish grammar.
They turned us from our natural tongue
with their regime, more than any tallystick,
always ready with the cat-of-nine-tails, their *bataí*,
while us cats perpetually ran out of nine lives.
And now the cats are out of the bag
we'll let all that catty, clergy-bashing old hat go.
Besides there were good ones too: Sister Patrick,
Brother Pius, Fabian, and Brother William — who chucked it,

and according to the bible of rumor, shacked up with a nun.
And oh, John O'Shea who could read poetry aloud
better than anyone and still can and does . . . all those
nourishing souls who blessed those hand-wringing days
and sent us on our not-so-merry, merry ways.

*

But I keep getting lost like our drive that day,
as if being lost is the actual right way,
taking our cue from the likes of Christy Columbus, Brendan,
Odysseus and Wrong Way Corrigan: that misdirected crew,
whose wrong ways turned out right.
Quod erat demonstrandum: the right way
being the lost way and the long way round
being the only way home, it being home.

*

All I set out to say was what has stayed with me
of that day and that drive home is how I had,
corny as it sounds, a sort of epiphany:
the snowflakes scattering into the lights
were not tatters of a torn exercise page that correcting
Brother Dermot, Sister Benedict or any of the poetry heads
tore in disgust and cast all abaa in the darkening classroom
that falling snow reminded me of earlier.
No: rather it was the inverse of the sins
of our childhood that blew over our tongues
and souls like the soot of bonfire night,
coating all the windows of our city.
The snow was manna falling
as good a symbol as any of the nourishing company
and gab of our day, knowing with all the darkness
crowding our vision, that we were blessed too
what with our families, friends and the miracle of miracles:
poetry, shagging poetry, I kid you not,
lucky enough to have come this way.

The snow fell in the silence that poetry
falls with as it drops a beneficence of
white calmness around us in the darkness.

*

The next thing I recall, as we snail-paced down
from the White Mountains, was finally finding
our bearings at a crossroads with a shellityhorn-spired,
picture postcard New England church
somewhere near Morrisville that, when my friend
Chuck lived there, I nicknamed Nowheresville.

At first we thought there was something wrong,
an accident, seeing what looked like a father and son
out of their pick-up, sprawling at the roadside,
moving their arms and legs as if writhing in pain.
But then it dawned on me they were making angels,
signing their body's X signatures in a snow mound.
They might have been aping early pioneers of flight,
Dedalus and Icarus making a myth of that myth,
finally copping that their escape plan is for the birds
and never again wanting to leave the blessèd earth.

WE WILL NOT PLAY THE HARP BACKWARD NOW, NO

If in Ireland
they play the harp backward at need

Marianne Moore, 'Spenser's Ireland'

We, a bunch of greencard Irish,
    vamp it under the cathedral arches
    of Brooklyn Bridge that's strung like a harp.
But we'll not play
the harp backward now, harping on
      about those Micks who fashioned
this American wind lyre
and about the scores
        who landed on Ellis Island
or, like us, at Kennedy and dispersed
through this open sesame land

in different directions like the rays
    of Liberty's crown, each ray
    forming a wedge or caret.
We'll refrain from inserting
how any of us craved for the old country
      and in our longing, composed a harp,
pipe, porter and colleen Tir na nÓg.
And if we play
      the harp right way round now
we'll reveal another side of the story
told like the secret of Labraid the Exile: how

some, at least, found a native genius for union
    here, and where, like the Earl Gerald,
    who turned himself into a stag
and a green-eyed cat
of the mountain, many of us
      learned the trick
of turning ourselves into ourselves,
free in the *fe fiada* anonymity
      of America. Here
we could flap the horse's ears
of our singularity and not have to fear,

nor hide from the all-seeing Irish
    small town, blinking evil eyes.
    Nor does this landscape play that unheard,
but distinctly audible
mizzling slow air
      that strickens us with the plaintive notes
of the drawn-out tragedy
of the old country's sorry history.
        No, we'll not play the harp backward
any more, keeping in mind the little people's harp
and how those who hear it never live long afterward.

From the poem 'THE HELLBOX'

When push comes to shove, more than anything
I didn't want to feel a foreigner
in my own, what would you call it, homeland?,
or just the *Old Country*, as here they label
anywhere across the drink and that I still,
circa a decade later, surprise myself
in casual conversation by calling *home*.
My home city, emigrating from itself, changed
so hell for leather, even if it was for the better,
that some of us felt oddly abandoned. Our one-time dark
side streets turned into trendy shopping thoroughfares:
Paul Street, French Church Street, Half Moon Street,
Carey's Lane, where after Kojak's Nightclub
I pulled off the occasional guilt-ridden feel,
even managed the odd fumbling dry ride.
And I'll say little of how aliens like Burgerlands
and McDonald's took over main streets and buildings
in the continuous sci-fi movie of our century,
nor about the twilight zone, routing roads
that the Cork Corporation calls *da Super Highway*,
motoring over fields, woods and railway lines that still
hoot and whistle inside me down the sleepers of the years
and where we played the Easter Rising. I was
fierce Pearse, wheelchair Connolly and Cork's own Big Fella,
never Joseph *Mary* Plunkett, wearing my cowboy hat
pinned to one side Volunteer-style; though reluctantly
I took my turn at being an executing Tommy.

On other days we played Cowboys and Indians.
I was always the lone redskin brave having written
in my Santa letter one misdirected Christmas
for an Indian suit with a set of Big Chief feathers
colorful as a macaw or a bird of paradise,
spotted in Kilgrew's Toy Shop that's shot now also,
all gone Baker's John along with the aroma
of Thompson's bakery rising like dough over the Lee.
The mane of on-the-warpath feathers trailed gloriously
or flapped mid-air all those times I was hunted and fired at
as I rode Injun style, wishing there were more Indians
and I didn't all the time have to be the sole baddy
and that one of the cavalry would swap outfits,
and let me be a paleface, but no one ever did.

And who else could they chase? I've this notion that
that lonesome whooping, bow and arrow Apache,
always staying one step ahead of the posse,
eventually camped way up the line in a hideout
writing his smoke-signal poems on the sky.

From the translation of Aristophanes, *The Suits* (1999)
(retitled from *The Knights*), revised 2017

(The chorus begins to dance in a circle)

Strophe
Ladies and gentlemen, it's chorus time, and we admit —
since you're all such aficionados of comedy and wit —
that had any comic writer of the old days
begged us to take part in one of his plays,
it's dubious, frankly, he'd have had a chance.
But this chap, this maker, shares our stance.
He speaks right up and doesn't try to dupe   270
the truth, even if it'll land him in the soup.
Has any of you ever heard of his name?
You look cagey. You wonder what's his game?
Why has he hidden in the wings for so long?
He's asked me to explain how, all along,
he's intentionally avoided the public eye.
He knows his craft is, without a word of a lie,
the toughest of all the arts to pull off.
He knows to boot, now don't laugh or cough,
that the audience's taste can quickly grow cold.   280
You dump many as soon as they've grown old.
Look at poor Magnes. He was your favorite,
but as soon as his hair greyed, he didn't rate.
He won all the awards and prizes of his day.
He performed the flute for you in every way,
played the birds, Lydians, mosquitos, even a frog.
But as soon as he lost it, you treated him like a dog.
And what about poor, unfortunate Cratinus.
He swept the country with success after success.

Antistrophe
His were the only ditties heard at any sing-along.   290
Staves like "Stupendous Composers of Great Song"
or "Toro, the Thief, Who Didn't Give a Fig."
These days you refuse to give him a sideshow gig.
Now his voice is kaput and his harp out of tune
you don't give a damn. You won't grant him a boon.
He staggers about, mindless from booze,
parading his pathetic, bedraggled garland prize.
He's so far gone he'd drink out of a slave's boot,
while to honor him — even now you don't give a hoot —
he should be given a seat high up in the gods,   300

along with all the politicians and their broads.
And what about Crates, our sorry, old comic?
He concocted his own subtle word-tonic.
And even if at times he was somewhat off,
it was a bit harsh of you, perhaps, to scoff.
So, surely you understand the predicament
of this artist, wisely wary of such treatment.
Besides, he believes one should know one's craft,
from the bow all the way aft,
before setting out on the treacherous ocean.   310
Honestly, don't you think such precaution
is laudable? He didn't sail in here all swagger,
perched at the stern, another blasted bragger.
So come on, raise a wave of applause his way.
Grant this maker a safe haven in our bay.

[...]

CHORUS
    Welcome back. What a brick.
    We've been worried sick.   360
    Did you best the tricky chick?
    Tell us the story quick.

SAUSAGE FINGERS
    Sure. No problem. I whacked her.

CHORUS (surrounding him and dancing)
    Well now, three cheers.
    You are some bucko.
    You've spoken well before,
    but please, we're mad to know
    what you said. You've nothing to hide.
    We are all on your side.   370

SAUSAGE FINGERS
Well, wait till you hear this. You'll get a kick out of it.
    As you know, I legged it to the ass-embly and
    got there right on her heels. She was already up
    to her tricks, spreading lies about us all.
    Madam Ass-licking Innocent, herself. The
    whole assembly was agog and aghast. She
    smeared the mustard on thick and fast.

When I saw the assembly, swayed by her smear
        campaign, being reeled in hook, line,
        and sinker, I figured that it was time to act.
I said a quick prayer along the lines of, "By all the
        hoodwinking powers of chicanery, deceit, and
        fraud, all those that shaped my childhood,
        she's not going to trump me. Bless
        my tongue with blarney and ballyhoo."
I'd hardly finished mumbling the prayer when some
        character left a humongous fart to my left.
        Right, I say, the wind's on my side,
        so I squeezed myself through and let go:
        "Members of the assembly let me be
        the first to tell you the tremendous news that
        the war has helped slash the price of small fry."
You should have seen their gobsmacked faces. They
        could have kissed me, each and every one of 'em.
Then, to really land them, I leaked that they should buy
        every frying pan in town, so no one else could
        fry up. They leaped up in a wave of applause.
        They were speechless. They opened and closed
        their mouths like dumb fish. I caught them, alright.
I knew Papclinton was no fool either. She knew my game,
        and knew what the assembly wanted also. She piped up:
        "Gentlemen, in the light of this fishy
        news, let's offer a hundred oxen to the goddess
        in appreciation." The assembly took the bait.
As soon as I realized what this piranha was up to, I hollered:
        "Let's offer two hundred." I suggested that
        they should sacrifice a thousand goats as well
        to Artemis, but only if sardines were still the
        same price. I hooked the assembly again, and drew
        them in.
She lost it as soon as she heard this. She made a lurch
        for me. The guards barely managed to drag her off.
        All the assembly were on their feet, nattering about the
        stinking situation.
She begged them to hold off and hear what the delegation from
        Sparta had to say about a peace treaty. But, in unison,
        they all hollered: "A peace treaty! Are you joking? They
        only want peace now that sardines are so cheap. They
        can do a running jump. Let the war continue.   380

They called a halt to the debate and scattered. I rushed to the
    market to buy up all the leeks in sight. I divvied them
    out to everyone I bumped into on the hill, gratis, as
    seasoning for their sardines. They were over the moon,
    thought the sun shone out of my ass.
I won the assembly over completely and with only a few
    leeks.

CHORUS
    You were born under a lucky star.
    You are bound to go far.
    You've outdone her in chicanery and bullshit.
    But don't rest on your laurels. Watch it.
    We're right behind you, old chap.   390
    Now run her off the face of the map.

*(The circle opens and retreats behind Sausage Fingers as
 Papclinton enters.)*

From the translation of Euripides, *Orestes* (1999) –
to be retitled *The Family*, or *Humankind*

CHORUS
The grand posterity,
the mighty prowess   400
flowing through Greece,
and on by the banks of Simois,
has ebbed again
and its waters have turned
bloody,
          polluted
from its source.
The house of Tantalus
was cursed after the feud
of the golden-fleeced lamb.
What followed from that   410
was the most gory banquet:
a feast of slaughtered princes;
tragedy after bloody tragedy
submerging the heirs of Atreus.
What seemed right
turned dreadfully wrong
as soon as it was done.
To slash a mother's throat,
raise the righteous blade
dripping in the sunlight   420
with her dark blood,
is perverted, and anyone
who thinks otherwise is mad.

At the end, Tyndareus' daughter
cried out again and again,
terrified of death: "No, my son,
no, if you murder your mother
you'll lose everything.
In revenging your father
you'll wrap your name   430
in eternal flames of shame!"

What affliction is more terrible?
What other tragedy
could match a son
steeping his hands
in the blood of his *own* mother?
For his crime, the Furies
furiously torment him

and drive him berserk. 440
Agamemnon's very own offspring
is unable to escape.
His eyes roll wildly,
those same eyes that beheld
his mother bare her breast to him
through gold-embroidered clothes.
He stabbed her there
with his own hand.
The wrong done his father
had wet the brand. 450

(Enter Electra.)

From *The Fifth Province* (2000)

AMERICAN WAKE

A breeze of turf catches me out
   of the hydrangea-blue sky
as I lollygag along a boreen,
   lovely as the brine on the wind,
simplifying this island.
   It's the whiff of memory, the memory
of memory lost, reaching down
   to the deserted famine village,
breaking the hearts of ghosts
   waving handkerchiefs of whitethorn
from gaping windows across the eternity
   of the spangling Atlantic.

FILM DIRECTIONS FOR THE UNDERWORLD

I recall Cocteau's black and white
surreal film of a descent to Hades
as our jet banks in early winter darkness.

We drop into rush-hour Manhattan,
a volcano spouting countless lava streams
of headlight traffic, pouring to the outskirts over

the Lethe of the East River and Hudson.
Come morning, the city will rewind fiery
taillight magma back into itself.

          *

To go on with this malarkey's too easy.
There's no scenario more suited for some wacky movie
of a descent into a contemporary underworld

than this metropolis. If anything
it's more like the otherworld of Irish myth
whose entrance is *Teach Duinn*, Bull Island,

off Cork and Kerry, my old homesteads.
Whatever region the souls descend to
is shrouded in perpetual mist.

          *

I've a hunch the Irish underworld is the realm
of the emigrant. After exiles are waked, they can't
shake the notion they've somehow passed on.

How many of those shades have disembarked
on this island after the limbo
of Ellis Island or Kennedy Airport?

They wonder, agog and aghast, how the hell
they've ended up wandering its canyon streets
without a clue, a foggy notion, a bull's.

They feel like extras in a movie, half-expecting
to see a giant gorilla swinging off the Empire State
or a star hanging by his fingertips from Liberty's torch,

unable to shake the sense
that at any moment they could step out of
the film, out of the cinema and swan

about the Grand Parade, O'Connell Street,
or Eyre Square and feel at home again, cursing
the eternal static screen of Irish rain.

*

I have this overhead shot of myself bag-slinging down
the accordion tunnel off a jet into an airport,
and though I knew no one would show up,

I still glanced round, hoping someone would be there
to welcome and guide me, or some stranger
holding my name up on a cardboard sign

like that Whitman-bearded guy held a name
printed in emerald letters. But there was nobody
to meet this lone green gringo off the stagecoach.

*

I lugged bags through the hubbub
of hugs and cameras, overwhelmed
by the twilight zone

of the sprawling city outside,
wishing someone would press
rewind and persuade the makers

that the film doesn't
have to follow the trend where every hit
has to have the predictable unhappy end.

From *The Blind Stitch* (2001)

TO MY MOTHER, EILEEN

I'm threading the eye
   of the needle for you again. That is
my specially appointed task, my
      gift that you gave me. Ma, watch me slip this
      camel of words through. Yes,
rich we are still even if your needlework
   has long since gone with the rag-and-bone man
     and Da never came home one day, our Dan.
   Work Work Work. Lose yourself in work.
    That's what he'd say.
     Okay okay.
Ma, listen I can hear the sticks of our fire spit
   like corn turning into popcorn
     with the brown insides of rotten teeth. We sit
in our old Slieve Mish house. Norman is just born.
   He's in the pen.
I raise the needle to the light and lick the thread
     to stiffen the limp words. I
peer through the eye, focus, put everything out of my head.
   I shut my right eye and thread.
I'm important now, a likely lad, instead
   of the *amadán* at Dread School. I have the eye
    haven't I, the knack?
   I'm Prince Threader. I missed it that try.
    Concentrate. Concentrate. Enough yacketty yak.
There, there, Ma, look, here's the threaded needle back.

ELEGY FOR AN AUNT

You'd not credit it, but tonight I lost my way and there wasn't a sinner
    to direct me
in the maze of alleys narrower than the lanes off Cork's norrie quays,
    and as manky,
when around one corner trots a funeral of Hindus with fanny-all on but
    their dhoti baydinahs.

I stepped aside from pallbearers shouldering a tinsel-covered body
    about the size of Kitty's,
whose bier I bore only weeks ago on the hills down to the ghats
of chemical factories lining the Lee, our Ganges.

I can still feel the dead weight imprinting my right shoulder and
    glimpse
taspy Joe out of badinage and a laugh, backed to the church wall.
We all sussed another of the old world souls was cut from us, as Rosy
    was and Noel and

and and, and with each *and* a subtraction as if we're disappearing ourselves
limb by phantom limb. Soon we'll be nothing but air.

✳

As the dolorous bearers wound their way, it dawned on me, if I followed,
they'd lead me to my lodgings above the burning ghat. Trailing, I felt
like an aish who tags a funeral through streets at home for free drink.

I doubt I could have gone farther from whatever home is under the embers
    of the Indian night
as I dekkoed a mourner scrawl the ash tilak of his dead before he swept
    the remains into
the heaven of the Ganges; the wherever of the hereafter.

✳

Now monkeys lumber and loaf on the balcony outside my room above
    the cremation's glow.
I still smell of pall smoke and my eyes water as they strain to follow
    my pencil,
this jotting the leaded shade of smarting smoke and ashes below.

THE STILT FISHERMAN
for Jonathan Williams

How glad I am
to have come to this out-of-the-way island
— ditching the hubbub of the city
with its pubs and cafés and my literati buddies —
seeking enlightenment by way of a woman.

And even if that's out of the question,
even if we can't know the world through each other,
going our separate ways, I understand why
Muslim sailors called this the Isle of Serendip
as I come upon a stilt fisherman
simply clad in a white lunghi
sitting on the perch of his stilt,
steadfast among the breakers.

*

He swings the lasso of his line
and waves me away as I swim to him,
scaring off the fish, buoyant in my stupidity.

*

Now he winds in a shimmering seerfish
and dunks it into his stilt's mesh bag.
He gives thanks, asks forgiveness of the seer.
The ocean in the swell of a wave
washes in around him.

*

I too am supplicant,
having wasted so much time,
all my life it seems,
fishing to be known.

Combers furl and fall
with the boom
of tall drums I heard at dawn
in the Temple of the Sacred Tooth,
played by bowing, anonymous men.

THE GECKO AND VASCO DA GAMA

The tangerine sun drops into the Arabian Sea. The colorful fishing boats are one-legged catamarans. Fruits bend the branches with luxuriant weight, pineapple and banana especially. Geckos play who-can-stay-still-the-longest on trees I can't name. How strange. How odd we are to one another, and after all these years. Boats settle down to fish for the night under tilly lamps defining darkness. The town lights of Vasco da Gama off along the Indian coast glimmer like the portals of a docked ship, allowing sailors shore-leave to become familiar again with their wives, their families, their aloneness. We'll stop here a while.

BEHOLD THE BRAHMINY KITE

That the Brahminy Kite shares the name of a god is not improper,
with its rufous body the tincture of Varkala's cliffs and white head
  matching the combers.
The kite riffs, banks and spirals; flapping black-tipped wings
mighty as the wings of the skate who might be the bird's shade in the
  stilly water.
The Brahminy makes light of the wind and circles the salt-and-pepper
  minarets of Odayam Mosque
rising above the palms and the silence-made-susurrus of the
  Lakshadweep Sea.
Now the kite is a silhouette in the glare of the sun, reminding me of
  vultures
above the hidden Towers of Silence that Patti and I spotted from the
  Hanging Gardens.
They dined off the cadavers of followers of Zarathustra himself.
And in my way I too believe in the kasti — the sacred thread — of the
  elements
stitching us all together, and would rather the kite pluck the flesh from
  my bones
than be laid in the dolled-up box of the West. When the time comes,
  imagine me the grub of the Brahminy.
Keep your elegy eye on the bird a day or so. Watch the kite make
  nothing of me.
Then, as I have now, give the Brahminy an almost imperceptible nod
  and turn and go.

PRAYER TO SAINT BLAISE

The Buddhist monks are up chanting and pounding their two-sided
   drums.
They've been at it since before dawn across the sanctuary of the lake
in the Temple of the Sacred Tooth, praying to the molar of Buddha.
Lately I find myself mumbling a Hail Mary or Our Father on the quiet,
as I did in the old, short pants days when I thought I was a goner if I
   missed spelling,
was late for school or confessed to impure thoughts about the Clark
   sisters, but now
I'm in trouble deep and childhood's terrors couldn't hold a candle to it.
   What matter
what the trouble is. We all know trouble — the royal trouble. The candle
   of middle age gutters down
to a malaise of disappointment about the whole hocus-pocus,
   holus-bolus ball of wax, even poesy —
I've lingered too long in the underworld of the poetry circle, another
   jostling jongleur jockeying to sup
from the blood of fame, or rather the ketchup, my ailing throat desperate
   to be heard.

                                   *

Now I swear I'll beeline to the Holy Trinity or whatever chapel when
   I'm back in the country of churches.
I'll not care a damn if any bookish crony spots me dip my hand in the
   font
as I slip inside to kneel among the head-scarved women lighting votive
   candles,
each beseeching a special saint for whatever ordinary miracle.

I will light a candle at some side-altar, Saint Blaise preferably.
On his feast day I'll queue up for the X of a pair of crossed candles to
   wax my throat
in the hands of a priest lisping the Latin blessing that my voice box not
   fail.
Sound. I'll chance this. I'll come again to poetry pax. I'll kneel before my
   childhood's sacred tooth.

THE PHONE BIRD

For days I've stayed within range of the phone,
    tethered to my need the way the phone is tethered
        to itself. Some days I listen so hard
            I'm sure I hear it ring.
When anyone calls, they're dumbstruck
    as my shaky greeting turns to despondency.
I admit that if you rang there'd be times
    you'd get an earful for not ringing.
        You know how I brood, turned in
on myself, willing the snake-coiled phone to ring,
    the handset clamped like devouring jaws on the rest.
Now the phone's a sleeping bird with its head tucked
    back in its wing. If you call,
I'll unfurl its neck and tenderly, tenderly I'll sing.

WHITE WORRY

He mentioned his box of white noise, how
    he turns on this constant low-level static
to drown out local fighter jets on maneuver; the news
    channel permanently on next door; the snarl
of chainsaws devouring the sometime forest
    reduced now to a wood, closing on our back gardens;
the siren and hooting street traffic; all the rest
    of the relentless, varying normal din.
At first, I thought how superfluous, how modern
    such contraptions are, but who am I to talk?
Look how I rely on low-level worries: the phone bill,
    a snub, something I ought to have said —
all my dear white noise switched habitually on,
    the reliable buzz in my head shrouding daily black noise.

INTERNATIONAL CALL

A hand holds a receiver out a top-storey window
in a darkening city. The phone is the black,
old heavy type. From outside
what can we make of such an event?
The hand, which seems to be a woman's,
holds the phone away from her lover, refusing
to let him answer his high-powered business call.
More likely a mother has got one more
sky-high phone bill and in a tantrum warns
her phone-happy son she'll toss the contraption.
A demented widow, having cracked the number
to the afterlife, holds the receiver out
for the ghost of her lately deceased husband.
He's weary of heaven and wants to hear dusk birds,
particularly the excited choir of city starlings.
It's always dusk now, but the receiver isn't held out·
to listen to the birds of the Earth from Heaven.
It's the black ear and mouth in the hand of a woman
as she asks her emigrated sisters and brothers
in a distant country if they can hear the strafing,
and those muffled thuds, how the last thud
made nothing of the hospital where they were slapped
into life. The hand withdraws. The window bangs closed.
The city is shut out. Inside now, the replaced phone
represses a moan. Its ear to the cradle
listens for something approaching from far off.

TAGGING THE STEALER
to David Cavanagh

So much of it I hadn't a bull's notion of
and like the usual ignoramus who casts his eyes
at, say, a Jackson Pollock or "This is just to say",
I scoffed at it. I didn't twig how it was as close
to art as art itself with its pre-game ballyhoo,
antics, rhubarbs, scheming, luck; its look
as if little or nothing is going on.
How often have we waited for the magic
in the hands of some flipper throwing a slider,
sinker, jug-handle, submarine, knuckle or screwball?
If we're lucky, the slugger hits a daisy cutter
with a choke-up or connects with a Baltimore chop
and a ball hawk catches a can of corn
with a basket catch and the ball rounds the horn —
Oh, look, Davo, how I'm sent sailing
right out of the ball park just by its lingo.
But I swear the most memorable play I witnessed
was with you on our highstools in the Daily Planet
as we slugged our Saturday night elixirs.
The Yankees were playing your Toronto Blue Jays.
They were tied at the top of the 9th.
I can't now for the life of me remember
who won, nor the name of the catcher, except
he was an unknown, yet no rookie.
Suddenly behind the pinch hitter's back he signaled
the pitcher. Seconds later the catcher fireballed
the potato to the first baseman, tagging
the stealer. It doesn't sound like much,
but everyone stood up round the house Ruth built
like hairs on the back of the neck, because the magic
was scary too. Jesus, give each of us just once
a poem the equal of that unknown man's talking hand.

THE BLIND STITCH

I can't say why rightly, but suddenly it's clear once more
    what holds us together as we sit, recumbent in the old ease
of each other's company, chewing the rag about friends,
    a poem we loved and such-like. Your Portuguese skin,
set off by a turquoise dress, doesn't hinder either.
    But there's something more than tan-deep between us.
I sew a button to a vest you made me, raveled years ago.
    You hemmed it with the stitch you mend a frock with now.
Our hands, without thought for individual movements, sew in
    and out, entering and leaving at one and the same time.
If truth be told, the thread had frayed between us, unnoticed,
    except for the odd rip. But as we sew, love is
in the mending, and though nothing's said, we feel it
    in a lightness of mood, our ease, our blind stitch.

From *The Ship of Birth* (2003)

THE ALIEN

I'm back again scrutinizing the Milky Way
    of your ultrasound, scanning the dark
      matter, the nothingness, that now the heads say
    is chockablock with quarks and squarks,
gravitons and gravatini, photons and photinos. Our sprout,

who art there inside the spacecraft
    of your Ma, the time capsule of this printout,
      hurling and whirling towards us, it's all daft
    on this earth. Our alien who art in the heavens,
our Martian, our little green man, we're anxious

to make contact, to ask divers questions
    about the heavendom you hail from, to discuss
      the whole shebang of the beginning and end,
    the pre-big bang untime before you forget the why
and lie of thy first place. And, our friend,

to say Welcome, that we mean no harm, we'd die
    for you even, that we pray you're not here
      to subdue us, that we'd put away
    our ray guns, missiles, attitude and share
our world with you, little big head, if only you stay.

THE AIR DISPLAY

Squadrons of geese fall-fly south, moving in
   and out of rank,
honking simply to stay together and to swap
   leader.
The teachers urge the children to look at fighter
   jets, the deafening Thunderbirds,
a name taken from the great Indian spirit, but
   nothing is said of that provenance.
The new god rips open the tepee vault of the sky
   above our schools and homes.
No one points out the caret of geese inserting
   themselves peacefully on the day,
or mentions what exactly the Thunderbirds
   mean to insert.
The geese unravel their chevron ranks, their echelon
   formation and, as if in civil disobedience,
reform again, but this time into a child's copybook
   correct sign.

THE SEAHORSE FAMILY

The seahorse is a question mark in the ark of the ocean
    that's carried it without question all this way.
Mythical as a unicorn, and even less believable,
    with its dragon head, its body a legless horse
        perpetually rearing, its monkey tail
    mooring it to sea grass, sponge or coral,
but, my mate,
    no stranger than who you are to yourself
    feeling large as a whale and small as a human.
Today I'd have us be seahorses, and I,
    being the male, would be the one in the family way.
I'd lug our hippocampus, *capall mara*, our shy seapony,
    our question mark anchored in you,
unquestionably unfurling its self day by tidal day.

HERO'S RETURN

Most people are caught up in the snow-mobbed day.
   Some are even ecstatic, the snow
      is still, after all, a novelty, a show
         getting under way.
Others are already dismayed,
   cursing impassable streets, traffic delayed
      and the general disarray
of winter giving itself its own ticker tape parade.

SNOW AND WIND CANTICLE TO AN UNBORN CHILD

Now the morning snowstorm is a swarm
of white locusts, not a biblical black wind
devouring all before it, but a charm
of benign creatures whose seeming simple end
is to becalm, dropping a bright humility
on the world, bringing the city to a stand-
still, turning their wings into a white sea
of, when walked on, what sounds like soft sand
that gets piled in snow combers or cotton candy,
or shaped into a button-eyed, carrot-nosed fatso.
Our plump snowman, whose eyes are still as blind
as buttons, soon we'll show you this and so
much more; how now what is called wind
blows a snow kiss, invisible as they say God is.

THE PRESENT

to Patricia Ferreira

Sparrows mostly, but chickadees,
cardinals, blue jays, wild canaries
feed all day on our bird-house stairs.
Sunflower seeds, beautiful black tears
your father gave us only a year ago.
He is dead now. How were we to know?
Snow is a white sheet laid silently upon
the body of the earth. How the dead live on.

BLACK SNOW

David points at the two-day snow bunkers along Broadway,
    not the natural jaundiced yellow of melting slush,
but as if a storm of smog-snow had fallen.
    He remarks: "That's what we breathe in every day,"
reminding me of how the nuns described the soul
    as a flake of snow and every trespass soot-darkens
that whiteness of whiteness. Ah, the soul of the world
    is made manifest to us today on Broadway and 82nd,
a fuming black exhausted snow-soul, woebegone
    as a bewildered oil-slick bird unable to fly.
I laugh, not without cynicism and apathetic stoicism, qualities
    necessary these days to survive, or rather, to get by.

FROM WOODY'S RESTAURANT, MIDDLEBURY

Today, noon, a young macho friendly waiter and three diners,
    business types — two males, one female —
are in a quandary about the name of the duck paddling
    Otter Creek,
the duck being brown, but too large to be a female mallard.
    They really
want to know, and I'm the human-watcher behind the nook
    of my table,
camouflaged by my stillness and nonchalant plumage.
    They really want to know.
This sighting I record in the back of my *Field Guide to People*.

A CIRCUS

I doubt anyone would've blinked if a ringmaster
marched in among us and this blarneying broadcaster
raised a megaphone to his lips, announcing
another highlight of the Greatest Show on Earth
along with the likes of the ball-bouncing,
baby-blubber seals; the hoop-leaping lemurs of mirth;
the tremendous, stupendous fandango of horses;
highflying doctors; funambulist nurses;
and all the farraginous farrago of this Earth,
not excluding me, the whistle-blowing clown,
the huffing and puffing red-faced Bozo father
of fathers, wearing a lugubrious frown,
cracking side-splitting sideshow banter
and flat-footed jokes, a sidekick to your mother.
The whole death-defying show spun out of order
as a drum roll hailed you: the debonair,
highflying, dare-devil god of the air,
none other than the Cannonball Kid himself,
shot from the dilatory, dilative distaff
opening of your ma, the human cannon herself,
lit a little over nine months ago by your father.
Your grey jump suit was smeared with bloody gauze
as you landed in the hand-net of nurse and doctor;
the whole show agape in the pause before applause.

LATE ENTRY

The white sea of a record storm was just ploughed open;
great snow combers held back either side of the road.
There was the quality of the miraculous about the night,
a crossing over out of danger, a leavetaking
and an arrival. While your ma zipped the overnight bag,
I swabbed the breaking-waters that could've been spilt tea
on our kitchen floor. I pulled the car round to
the front, helped her in as a hooded figure scavenged
our recycle bin, our poor attempt to save the world.
I wanted to call out, say there's no need to scurry
away, a modern-day leper, but another spasm
of your overdue entry had me behind the wheel
and us off, only to be flagged down on Pearl Street
by a police road block. Two streets later a driver
in a blizzard of alcohol barred the way, refused
to allow us pass until his girlfriend implored him.
On making the hospital, the nurse assured us
you'd probably slept through it all: the groaning,
the shopping-cart's leper-rattle, the swarming police
brisk in the drama of who-knows-what crime,
the drunk man's swearing and so much I've forgotten
or totally missed in the white-out of your storming.

THE GREEN ROOM

Shades of the green room about this scenario.
You lounge beneath the drip of the chemo,
talking shop with others, some bald, some still blest
with their own mops of hair, making the best
of your body's flaw and a visitor's melodrama.
You slip in and out of your latest part: the nausea,
dry mouth, diarrhea, the poison's impact,
having to go back out and face the next act.
The nurse assures you that you look just fine
even in your wig, that you're eternally twenty-nine.
You perk up, introduce "My son, the poet" to everyone.
A bald lady asks, "Do your poems rhyme like that one —
Fear no more the heat o' the sun — we did in school?
Write us one like that." "Okeydoke," says I, playing the fool.

THE JOKER FAMILY

You took such care of your hair.
   Now it comes out in clumps. "Maybe
      my new grandson could spare
         a share,"
you joked, Barber Death breathing down your neck.
We're always joking, keeping something or other in check,
    the Joker Family.

Remember how we'd beg you to open the window
   of our grey, white-topped Ford Anglia? But no,
   a mere hairline window crack of in-rushing air
      would toss your hair.
How we sweltered on those eternal drives to Everywhere:
Ringabella, Redbarn, Castlegregory, Glenbeigh.

"Now look at the scenery while the weather's fine," you'd say,
"We'll stop soon and each have a 99," fixing your hair
   in the rear-view mirror in that special way.

                *

Lately, on a drive round the Ring, near Kenmare,
   I risked wisecracking how your wig
is almost as good as your own erstwhile hair,
     itself a look-alike periwig,
and that, at least, we can open the car window.
   How we all laughed — you also.
   How the winds blow.

THE WAVE

I slip away
   — never being a morning person, as you say —
leaving you crisp as fresh cornflakes, playing peekaboo
    with Dan. He can't find you.
   You're putting a good face on things. Fair dues.
Even if you don't quite know the test's full news.
   I think you know.
   How can we say your body is coming undone?
Isn't everyone?

A boat is shouldered across the dunes off Lamb's Head
   like a coffin. Where do you go when you're dead?
I'd pester you about that, not much older than Danno.

Already you're making ready.
   We watch from above. Your boat bobs insecurely.
Run up the sail. Let me lend you a hand. Show.
It's so clear on the horizon today
   and the water so calm beyond the bay.
You head out past Bird Island towards *Teach Duinn*.
   A quick getaway would be a boon.
   Dan has learned to wave now too.
    He'll never remember you.
Look Ma, my hand. You'll be out of sight soon.

SHOPPING FOR A COMPOSTER

Rooting around what simply looked like refuse bins
I sounded out the petite clerk. Opening an exhibit,
she picked up a rotting fruit to expose worms
covering the flesh. She talked of them naturally,
endearingly even. I'll try to take a leaf from this woman
who spoke of the mass of blood-red worms as if it was a rose,
and you fresh in the grave, and I unable to help
picture you, in your coffin dark, covered with such a posy
all the way from your roman nose to your pedicured toes.

THE SKUNK MOTHS

The family of skunks, their backs to me from our deck,
    are like great black and white caterpillars. I imagine them
the giant larvae of Luna moths or Monarch butterflies,
    their pupae unzipping, tremendous wings unfolding,
fluttering about the summer airways, big as people;
    each revanchist proboscis exacting retribution for those
we've not let flutter down the summers. Imagine
    their eyes, big as cow eyes, gazing, gazing at us.
Imagine the Luna's gossamer tulle wings, the tippets
    brushing us, fanning us tenderly, wrapping us in a veil,
bringing us gently to our knees in a gathering humility,
    brushing aside our mortification, finally at home, natural
in the natural world — their wings our cocoon — becoming
    ourselves, pinioned resplendence, at last the human mothfly.

From translations of Kyriakos Charalambides,
Selected Poems (2005)

ICARUS

The sun
followed the contest.
Icarus plummeted
into his grave,
lost his radiance.

The sun turned pale,
the sea made a pact with the sun
and she kept the pact,
neither of them in a panic.

The sun plunged beneath the sea
where Icarus fell, but couldn't come up with the lad.
The sun emerged again at dawn
hoping to retrieve him some day.

THE APPLE

Picking the apple from the basket
brought to mind the rosy apple
of her child's cheek. Even now
he might be rotting
in jail.
The poor lad wasn't more than seventeen.
He hadn't even finished school,
nor gone into the army. He wouldn't kill a fly:
he was so polite, timid and innocent.

She put back the apple in the basket
recalling (they seemed so vivid to her)
other mothers like herself under the Turkocracy.

No one really gives a damn about her child
except for her, and the thousand others like her.
God be praised, there's not a word
for all the petitions and official statements,
for all the committees and UN envoys,
for all the politicians and government officials,
observers and votes, obligations and engagements,
conferences, solidarity, exhibits and funds.

Everything is organized to a tee
with conviction, special auditoriums, records —
yes, the motherly State takes care of all.

But the apple, the rosy apple in the basket.

GRECO-ROMAN CIVILIZATION

On a verdant plot by the river
stood the hippodrome of Corinth.
There, Nero of Nemea, Captain Tamer himself,
designed to test his strength,
or rather, rack up another victory.

So he mounts his chariot,
impetuous as ever. The unbeatable
Roman emperor charges off.

Bad luck; one of his steeds
suffers a sprain, but immediately the Greeks
replace it with another stalwart stallion.

Bad luck; his wheel buckles
and the hotshot Greeks intervene
and fit another wheel to his chariot.

Bad luck; the harness comes undone
and the horses shake free and stampede.
But the good Greeks, especially
all those competing with him,
immediately pull the reins of their chariots
and their horses brake.

Then the mighty emperor
descends to earth and crosses
the line on his own divine legs.
Thus he finishes first, as always,
sans his chariot — and so what?
He was a born conqueror,
unflinching before all peril.

The Greeks who are wise to such things,
madly cheer such a mighty feat.

If he weren't Roman, he'd like
to be a Greek, certainly — he wishes,
it seems, to flourish
in their logic and sound judgement: their applause
deserves a lowering of taxes,
the laurels they crown him with are worthy recognition

of a Roman citizen, certainly.

But not, by Zeus, their prolonged
thunderous ovations — the way they're going on
they'll walk off with the kingdom.

DEATH'S ART

King Cambyses, that Persian hard as granite,
was mad to humble
the Pharaoh Psammetichus,
his prisoner from Egypt.

He ordered that his old enemy
be placed in a cage of burnished silver
and set high above the Avenue of Lions.

The Pharaoh's daughter was paraded before him
lugging a water pitcher and with her breasts exposed
to torture him even more.

But the Egyptian remained a silent monolith,
his eyes fixed to the ground.

Cambyses, obstinate as ever, ordered
that the son of the Pharaoh be bound
and savagely dragged before his father's black eyes
on the way to being executed.

Still Psammetichus gazed stubbornly
at the ground, his silence imprinted
with an ant's humility, a snake's wisdom.

A long procession of shackled slaves
was filed before him.
A sole servant
was the only Egyptian martyr.

The Pharaoh broke into tears seeing this man,
his daughter and son too much for grief, beyond tears.

See how the Pharaoh prisoner
was so schooled in the art of death.

From the collection *Aceldama*,
published in *Collected Poems 1986–2006* (2006)

WASHING MY MOTHER

You inclined
your chemo'd head,
a few straggly wisps of grey.
The image in the mirror, a figure
experimented on by the Schutzstaffel
of regular life, worse in a way
for being so. But we must not say so.
I sponged your neck, the bra-seared markings of your back,
soaped down the knuckles of your spine,
shut out everything, showed not a sign.
"Is that okay?" thinking how you'd say
"I washed and powdered your bum many a day."
No laughs now, not even to relieve awkwardness.
You answered "Fine, love, fine."

THE LAST COIFFEUR

Nothing was stranger throughout the drear whirligig
of plans, condolences, humor-to-get-us-through
than the mortuary ringing, unsure how to fix your wig
so like your hair no one had a clue, or so we told you.
That I was your last cosmetologist played a hand
in my shaky hand. You, our cosmogony, wouldn't allow
even the meekest July zephyr ruffle a strand,
each precious wave curling on to your brow
like the blue-tinted wavelet-furling-on-wavelet
that you paddled through on holidays at Salthill,
Silver Strand, Rossbeigh, Banna, Myrtleville
— Ma, the water wasn't near as chilly as your brow —
and you, with your hands securing your hairnet,
crying to us in the deep: "You'll catch cold. Come in now."

IN TIMES OF WAR
while reading W. B. Yeats and Patrick Kavanagh

So, the monocled poet delights in the two Chinamen
seated there on the cracked, lofty lapis-blue slopes
under snow drops of cherry blossom. Their serving man
caresses plaintive strings as the wise hyperopes
in the cute little halfway house, sipping green tea,
stare on all the tragic scene; their ancient eyes glitter gay.
Over them flies the spindly-legged bird, Longevity,
croaking in the mind's ear all will be "Okay, Okay."
Elsewhere, a bit along the rocky slope and of a par,
another poet eulogizes geese flying in fair formation
to Inchicore, how their wings will out-wing the war.
Oh, my two poets I steer by, I know my station,
but what of the mother stooped over her child,
the wild pen over the limp cygnet, the pen defiled?

LOOSESTRIFE

You have become your name, loosestrife,
    carried on sheep, spurting up out of ballast,
a cure brought across the deep
    to treat wounds, soothe trouble.
There have been others like you, the rhododendron,
    the cattails that you in your turn overrun.
Voices praise your magenta spread, your ability
    to propagate by seed, by stem, by root
and how you adjust to light, to soil, spreading
    your glory across the earth even as you kill
by boat, by air, by land all before you: the hardy iris,
    the rare orchids, the spawning ground of fish.
You'll overtake the earth and destroy even yourself.
    Ah, our loosestrife, purple plague, beautiful us.

ESPERANTO

This morning a waiter in a Montmartre café
    was baffled by my attempt at his language.
Everyone chimed in to translate, all strangers.
    The waiter got it, smiled
and everyone smiled. For a moment it was as if
    a great problem was solved, as if each registered
the answer we forgot we knew, the froth
    of goodwill bubbling up like cappuccino.

UR GOD

There's something about the gourd,
how each can look so absurd,
and so different from the other — compare
the egg gourd, say, with the turk's turban
or swan with the crown of thorns, pear,
caveman's club, dolphin, pumpkin,
or the serpent inciting sin
and knowledge. How could they be kin?

They're as various as their uses:
currencies, condoms, bird-houses,
marimbas — you name it. And the name,
the concealed god within; our
gourd whispering that we're all the same
beneath the rind, the god we scour
the earth for on our knees. Our word,
who art on earth, hallowed be thy gourd.

ACELDAMA

And Judas cast down the pieces of silver in the temple, and went and hanged himself. And the priests and elders took counsel, and bought with the pieces of silver the potter's field, to bury strangers in. Wherefore that field has been called Aceldama, Field of Blood, unto this day.

Matthew 27:5–8

We drove down what seemed the curve
of the earth, sandwiched in our Ford Anglia.
We were happy as the colors of our beachball,
a careless car full of mirth and singalong songs,
songs that were mostly as sappy
as the soppy tomato sandwiches sprinkled with sand,
which is why they're called sandwiches our father said,
sandwiched himself now in the ground between his mother
and ours. What's the meaning of dead?
Which one of us children asked that as we passed
the spot with the lit steel cross on Carr's Hill,
putting the kibosh on the next song,
our mother about to break into "Beautiful City"?
She crossed herself, saying that's the place they bury
those whose lives somehow went wrong, betrayed
in one way or other, without a song to their names,
or a name, everyone buried together
and alone without a headstone.
The crepuscular loneliness of the field
shrouded our bright time. Our world,
the city below, shimmered like the silver pieces
scattered on the dark floor of the temple.

From translations of poems by Seán Ó Ríordáin, (2007)

MY MOTHER'S BURIAL

June sun in the orchard,
   the silksusurrus of afternoon,
a damn bee droning,
   ululatearing afternoon's gown.

I pored over a tarnished old letter.
   Every sip
caught my breath,
   every piercing word drew a tear.

I remember the very hand that wrote this,
   a hand as familiar as a face,
a hand meek as an old bible,
   a hand that was a balm when sick.

And midsummer fell back into midwinter,
   the orchard became a white graveyard by the river.
In the center of the dumb whiteness
   the black hole cried out in the snow.

Brightness of a girl on her first communion,
   brightness of the host on a Sunday altar,
brightness of the milksilk ribboning from the breast
   as they buried my mother, brightness of the sod.

My mind was demented struggling
   to grasp the funeral
when out of the white silence a robin flew down
   gently, without fear, without confusion

and stayed above the grave as if aware
   of its errand, hidden from everybody,
except the body waiting in the coffin.
   I envied their extraordinary intimacy.

The air of paradise descended on the grave.
   The bird had a terrible saintly gaiety.
I was a man excluded from the secret affair,
   distanced from the grave.

Sorrow's fragrance washed my impure soul.
   Chastity's snow fell on my heart.

Now my heart is cleansed, I'll bury the memory
    of the woman who carried me in her womb.

The gravediggers appeared with shovels
    rigorously spading clay into the grave.
I looked away, a neighbor brushing his trouser knees,
    the worldliness on the priest's face.

June sun in the orchard,
    the silksusurrus of afternoon,
a damn bee droning,
    ululatearing afternoon's gown.

I'm writing little, lame verses.
    I'd like to grab hold of a robin's tail.
I'd like to scatter those knee scrubbers.
    I'd like to make my way, sadly, to the end of day.

BEHIND THE HOUSE

Tír na nÓg is behind the house,
    a fantastic, topsy-turvy place;
four-footed characters pace
    about without shirts or shoes,
    without English or Irish.

A cloak grows on each back
    in this hugger-mugger place,
a tongue's spoken behind the house
    no one could understand but Aesop
    and he's in the dust now.

There's hens and chickens;
    a steady, uncouth duck;
a great black dog hounding the land,
    snarling at everyone;
    and a cat milking the sun.

In the far corner there's a rubbish heap;
    all the wonders of the world lie there:
a candlestick; buckles; an old straw hat;
    a mute toy trumpet;
    and a white kettle like a goose.

It's there the gypsies come,
    saintly, harum-scarum,
kin to the back of the house;
    it's here they seek alms
    at the back of every home in Ireland.

I'd like to be behind the house
    in the darkness, late,
to witness, in the moonlight
    the scholarly pooka himself,
    Professor Aesop.

FOOTPRINTS

Now I'd like to meet him
when it's out of the question.
He went southwards that morning.
He'll never return.

A sunny morning in Kerry,
the skitting stream can be heard
like hidden girls' giggling in the gully
as I pass that way.

He walked with me that morning,
the pair of us on the one path.
It struck me walking back,
noticing his footprints in the mud,

that he wasn't here till he left.
Being here he can never be there.
That character who's gone
is a complete person.

May the soul of that fellow
who accompanied me,
and the souls of all my diverse selves
who follow, be saved for ever.

Those feet that printed the mud
were also mine, yet
it wasn't I who was the one with him
listening to the stream.

I wasn't born until he died.
There are many "me"s in myself.
I die with every word,
but I rise with every breath.

The new me tags me
until one becomes the other.
Myriads pen these verses,
a new person with every breath.

Layer by layer I peel
these characters from my heart.

It's no wonder I'm fond of the prints
in the mud as I depart.

CLAUSTROPHOBIA

Beside the wine
a candle, terror.
The statue of my Lord
appears without power.
What's left of night
teems into the yard;
the government of night
rules outside my window.
If my candle is snuffed,
later on, in spite of me,
the night will spring
into my lung;
my mind will be overwhelmed;
terror will smother me;
I'll become night;
I'll be a live dark:
but if my candle holds
a single night
I'll be a republic of light
until day dawns.

COLD SNAP

One icy morning I went out.
A handkerchief hung from a bush.
I reached to put it in my pocket.
Frozen, it slid from my grip.
It wasn't a stiff cloth slipped my grasp,
but something that died last night on a branch.
There I was, racking my brain
till snap, its match:
    that time I kissed a relative
    stretched in her coffin, petrified.

THE MOTHS

The sound of a fragile moth, a page turning,
the brushing of its winglets
in the bedroom, a night in autumn,
the torment of something frail.

Another night in a dream I felt
a pair of moth's wings,
expansive as the wings of an angel,
fragile as a female.

It was my role to handle them
and not let things go amiss,
to take them without harm
and bring them bliss.

But I spilt the blessed powder
finely sprinkled on each wing.
I figured I'd never be numbered
one of the cock-of-the-walk lads

who strutted straight out of my confusion
bragging, as usual, of their prowess,
scoring each other from one to ten.
Everyone, but myself, was in.

The sound of a fragile moth, a page turning,
the soiling of the moth film,
an autumn night and the moths fluttering.
I dwell too much on their minor commotion.

IN ABSENTIA

There's hardly anyone there.
Most are out of it.
Our concern and our care
is not in being there
    but not to feel the being there.

If being there wasn't so dull
why would we need to pass the time?
Why would we drink
except to be always out of it
    and never settle within ourselves?

Whatever else you wait for,
do not wait for your self.
Whatever you see,
don't see yourself above anyone else,
    to be blind to your own self is best.

What is fame or reputation worth?
Who'd be listening to you?
Who'll pass judgement on a poem
if everyone is outside of it
    except for Sweeney the madman?

The whole crew is on the run.
Everyone's running from themselves.
The whole lot are out of it.
Is there anyone, besides a saint, within
    the abandoned hearth of God?

FEVER

It's a steep climb from the bed.
The sickly sweltering mound
is a long way from the ground.
    Miles and miles away
    folks still sit and stand.

We're here in the terrain of sheets.
We can barely recall a chair.
    Once we stood sound on level ground,
    in a time of walking, long ago.
    We stood as tall as the window.

A picture swells off the wall.
The frame melts into a haze.
Reason can't stop it.
    Things close in around me,
    the world falls apart.

A locality is forming in the ether,
a parish perches on my finger.
I could easily grasp a chapel.
    There are cows on the road to the north.
    The cows of eternity are not as tranquil.

THE MAD WOMAN

Her distress is kindling since noon.
It'll persist till her mind blows.
The whole room is a tinder box.
She strikes the answers like matches off herself.
She'll be dispatched to the madhouse at first light;
the room, answers and herself finally snuffed out.

CLARITY

Last night I went on a drinking spree.
This morning I see the world clearly.
I can't recall a world so spick and span
as this one on the outskirts of our rantan.

There's not a word without clarity,
not a neck's crook, or a head's pole.
Here bottle is the essence of bottle —
everything becomes whole.

Everything is clear as day,
everyone's story.
For the first time it dawns on me
why it's all hunkydory.

RETURN AGAIN

Leave the mad world behind,
all that's coursing through us in this year of our Lord.
Put it out of your mind:
the Pale, the Battle of Kinsale. . . .
And, since the load's heavy
and the road long, untackle
the halter of the English Pegasus:
Shelley, Keats and Shakespeare.
Return again to what is us.
Ease your mind, relax
your mouth haltered in the syntax
that's thwarted your voice.
Make a clean breast of it.
Make peace with your own race,
with your own place.
It's not natural for anyone to ditch their own country.
On a bright afternoon take the cliff road to West Kerry.
On the horizon you'll catch sight
of the Collective Blaskets, the Subjunctive Skelligs,
the ancient school of Irish shoaling from mouths,
    that's your entry,
    Dún Chaoin in the evening light;
    knock and your true self
    will open sesame.

WORK

Work suits the sinner.
He needs it as a cover.
Without it he's naked.
What a thought.

APATHY IS OUT

There's not a fly, moth, bee,
man, or woman created by God
whose welfare's not our responsibility;
to ignore their predicament
isn't on.
There's not a madman in Gleann na nGealt
we shouldn't sit with
and keep company, since
he's sick in the head
on our behalf.

There's not a place, stream or bush,
however remote; or a flagstone
north, south, east or west
that we shouldn't consider
with affection and empathy.
No matter how far South Africa,
no matter how distant the moon,
they're part of us by right:
there's not a single spot anywhere
we're not a part of. We issue from everywhere.

CLIFFTOP, DUNQUIN, AUGUST 1970

This locality is saying something. If it could be put in words, then it would be known that this locality was saying something. The sea, the rocks, the grass, everything growing here says this is the way it is. The people say it. They say it when silent. It is what they say whether speaking or silent. Although it is not what they say. It would be a relief to hear it flushed out in words. It would be nothing new to us. It's said so forcefully by this locality that it must be examined from time to time. It is endurance.

From *The New Citizen Army* (2010)

THE NEW CITIZEN ARMY

Today, as every day, you rise up, don your suit,
   denims, dress — whatever fatigues
society rigs you out in. You'll be one among
   minions under orders.
You'll not think of it like this, you'll not
   think once. You'll eat breakfast,
hardly aware that long ago you were drafted,
   a soldier in the New Citizen Army.
This is as it should be; all regulars must be
   mindless in the execution of duty.
You'll drive to work: the office, the hospital,
   the university — wherever you make your living.
All day you will make your dying, a good taxpayer.
   After you arrive home, you settle back
on the couch, surf the news, the bodies laid out in neat rows,
   men, women, children, parents weeping.
The daily massacre. You have obeyed the command.
   You think nothing of it. You've played your part.
You are the good citizen. Sit back. Relax.

NEW OSTIA

The red glow of the burning city towered into the sky.
The fetus of terror stirred in us. To witness people in flames
leap from high windows, call out. Too much.
The old world brought down around our heads.
The aftermath a seething bewilderment.
Tribunes fan the sparks of public anxiety
into panic, dispatch soldiers to ports, stations,
set up roadblocks, search for weapons. Rumors
of another attack. Opposition cowed by accusations
of being soft, unpatriotic. Special measures called for.
A supreme commander set up
to combat threats, terrorist legions.
How a timorous population can be molded,
powers ceded to our Pompey Magnus
and his cronies, lining their already lined pockets.

ENTERING THE ACROPOLIS

In the temple of Athena Nike, the goddess smiles smugly
   down on the daily tourists in their comfortable Nikes.
She has won again. Not all victory is a matter of war. Complicity
   is the deity hardly anyone sees.

THE NOBLE LIE

I am a citizen of the country where truth
lies. Even now you shouldn't believe me.
I lie my private snow-white lies,
concocted excuses for being late,
harmless fibs to evade a row. Why
make anyone cry? I lie my public lies,
a citizen voting for lesser evils,
a taxpayer dropping the exploding lies
of democracy on unseen people.
The condoned lies of the public
become noble. A lie shared is
a lie made truth, easier to excuse
the black lie, grey lie, blue lie, green lie,
purple lie, yellow lie, the blood-red lie.

OSTRAKA

The eight winds blow,
an earthquake shakes Mount Olympus, cholera
ravages the states, drought everywhere, the mysterious
death of bees throughout the country,
the flowers and crops die, the hourly
slaughtering of innocents,
                                and all we do is debate
in the assembly, cast *ostraka* — shards of democracy —
regarding our ships, the color of their sails.

FAMILY OF MAN

The blood-red poppies grow in the ancient site,
    Agamemnon's headquarters, the fall of the house of Atreus,
one abomination leading to another down through the centuries
    since Thyestes made a meal of his own sons.
Are we in Mycenae, Flanders, Iraq, some war zone
    of the future? The poppy is the flowering myth
that flourishes everywhere on disturbed earth.

FOXED

At the limestone stadium hewn from the rock of Parnassus
    above Delphi's Oracle, the Games were held
to celebrate Apollo. Poets and philosophers traveled here
    to glorify the god, compete in their own way.
Today the Church of Sport and its high priests don't care
    an iota for poetry, deflect us
from thinking, from witnessing the ongoing blood sport
    even as it touts that the games are a pressure valve
to release tension, bond rival states. Ares, foxing so many.

FAMILY CREST

The two swordfish in the market are gawked at by all
    who pass. Parents coax wide-eyed children up to ogle.
One grinning family has a photograph taken alongside.
    Picture these noble knights of the sea being caught,
their bodies, great muscles, writhing on the deck.
    The fish could be the heraldic sword-crossed emblem
of a coat of arms, but their great lances
    are hacked off. All they could emblazon now
is the family *Homo sapiens*.

From *The Word Exchange: Anglo-Saxon Poems in Translation*
(2011)

THE WANDERER

The loner holds out for grace
— the maker's mercy — though full of care
he steers a course, forced to row
the freezing, fierce sea with bare hands,
take the exile's way; fate dictates.
The globe-trotter spoke, heedful of hardship,
of brutal battle, the death of kith and kin:
    "Often at first lick of light
I lament my sole way — no one left
to open my self up to wholly,
heart and soul. Sure, I know
it's the noble custom for an earl
to bind fast what's in his breast,
hoard inmost thoughts, think what he will.

    The weary mind can't fight fate,
nor will grim grit help.
Driven men often harbor
chill dread fast in their chests.
So I, at sea in my angst,
(wretched outcast from my land,
far from kind kindred) brace myself,
having buried my large-hearted lord
years back in black earth. Abject,
I wander winter-weary the icy waves,
longing for lost halls, a helping hand
far or near. Maybe I'll find
one who'd host me in the toasting hall,
who'd comfort me, friendless,
gladly entertain me. Many
know what cruel company sorrow can be
for a soul without a single mate;
exile's path holds him, not finished gold;
a frozen heart, not the world's wonders;
he recalls retainers, reaping treasure,
how in youth his lavish liege
feted and feasted him. All is history.

    He who lacks a good lord's
counsel knows this story:
whenever sorrow and sleep combine
the wretched recluse often dreams
that he is with his loyal lord.
He clasps and kisses him, lays

his hands and head on those knees, loves
the liberal ruler as in whilom days.

  As soon as the sober man wakes
he sees nothing but fallow furrows;
seabirds paddle and preen feathers;
snow and frost combine forces.
Then his heart weighs heavier, sore
for the lord, sorrow renewed.
He recalls friends from the past,
gladly greets them, feasts his eyes.
His mates swim in waves of memory.
Those fellows drift away in his mind,
barely utter a word. Down again,
this man knows he must cast
his harrowed heart over frigid waves.

  It's not hard to guess why in the world
my spirit's in such a stark state
as I consider the lives of those peers,
how they abruptly quit the halls,
the bold youth. In this way the world,
day after day, fails and falls.
For sure, no man's wise without his share
of winters in this world. He must be patient,
not too keen, not brash, not harsh,
not easily led, not foolhardy,
not timid, not all gusto, not greedy,
not too cocky till he knows life.
A person should take stock before a vow,
brace for action, be mindful
of the mind's twists and turns.

  The wise man knows how ghostly it will be
when all the world's wealth is wasted
as in many regions on Earth today,
the still-standing walls wind-wracked,
ice-bound; each edifice under snow.
The hailstones fall, the lords lie low,
no more revels, troops of gallant veterans
lie valiant by the wall. Some fell in battle,
borne away: one was borne by vultures
over the ocean; one the hoar wolf
wolfed down; another a noble laid in a cave
— his mien a death mask of grief.
So the Shaper laid the Earth waste,
until, bereft of human life,

the ancient works of giants stand empty.
　　Anyone who dwells on these battlements,
ponders each stage of our dark life,
will wisely survey the distant past,
the myriad struggles, and exclaim:
Where is the horse gone? The young bucks? The kind king?
Where is the banquet assembly gone? The merrymaking?
Night shrouds all as if nothing ever was.
Now all that is left of those veterans
is a tower wall ringed with serpent devils;
missiles slaughtered those who served,
weapons amassed for mass murder, an incredible end.
Hurricanes attack the rocky coast.
Snowstorms sheet the earth.
Winter's tumult (dark comes then,
nightshadows deepen) drives hailstorms
out of the north to try us sorely.
This earthly realm is fraught.
Fate changes everything under the sun.
Here wealth is brief, friendship brief,
man brief, kinship brief.
All human foundation falls to naught."
　　So spoke the man from his heart, musing apart.
Blest is he who holds true. No man should openly bare
his heart's hardships unless he knows the cure,
that is his great feat. It's well to seek solace
from the maker, our one security.

From *Loosestrife* (2011)

ON LISTENING TO THE WORLD NEWS AGAIN

So, these days one is dimly consoled with the thought
Hell, even the sun will eventually come to naught.

US

The snow cap of Mount Discovery is like a white hanky,
    the knots tied in four corners on the shiny dome
of a bald man at a blistering All-Ireland final.
    No one here knows what hurling is. A game played by the gods
when they deign to come down and enter the human body.
    Ares, that most unpopular of commanders in chief
even among his ruthless peers, has made this country his own.
    Two fighter jets on display scissor the sky's blue cloth
to shreds. They fly above our house in pastoral Vermont.
    People nearby cheer. We are far from home.

PATIENT

The snow has melted clean off the mountain.
   It's winter still. Yet another indication that Gaia
is in trouble, that things aren't sound.
   The rocky mountaintop shines
like the bald head of a woman after chemo
   who wills herself out of her hospital bed
to take in the trees, the squirrels, the commotion
   around town, sip beer in a dive, smile
at the child ogling her shiny head, wishing
   it didn't take all this dying to love life.

THE CARYATIDS IN THE ACROPOLIS

So when the ruling, puffed-up males
    boast this is Democracy's birthplace,
let them consider us, the silent stone females,
    faces erased, holding up the roof-beams of our race.

From *The Greek Anthology, Book XVII* (2012)
American edition: *Book Seventeen* (2015)

THE FIRST STORY

The email, telling a friend, *we're not too bad considering*
    the state of the world, crosses the Atlantic
with the touch of a key. The leaves of an evergreen blow
    like a shoal of emerald fish returning to the same place.
A cardinal in his scarlet robe pecks the feeder.
    The bells of the Angelus ring from St Joseph's.
The Angel of the Lord declares unto Mary, the infant god
    of my childhood is back on earth again, the one
I've ceased to believe in, the lifebelt that keeps believers afloat
    in the storm of being here, issuing tickets to
the hereafter ever since that garden episode, the tall tale
    of our banishment concocted by some storyteller
who'd be so flummoxed we've taken it for gospel
    would say: "Look around you now. Behold, the garden."

                                  — Grigorographos

FALL OUT

Today I read a poet's elegy for his friend
    written forty years ago after he passed away.
It hurt me to read, how friendship still shone,
    a paradigm of friendlove, the jewel
in the crown of life. And I thought of you,
    and wished I was that poet, and you had died
in the good old days, and it was I that wrote that poem
    to you, my friend, my sometime friend.

— Gregory of Corkus

PARTY PIECE

Often the get-together is unavoidable:
    a marriage, funeral, function.
You brace yourself, most people being more
    friendly acquaintances than acquainted friends
— even with the latter you're more at ease meeting one
    at a time, tuning into each other's frequency.
You tire of shop talk, gossip, sports babble,
    politics, nervy jokes you laugh at too soon.
Tell yourself not to drink too much or your party mask
    will slip as you balance on the social pergola,
or rather the unsteady plinth of society, the necessary base.

                         — Gregory of Corkus

COMPANY

A secluded table in a café affords me a modicum
    of privacy. I settle down to read, work
among clusters talking about whatever folks
    talk about in a café. It's easy to feel warmth,
love even, towards others from this vantage.
    My jacket reserves the nearest chair
for my imminent friend, putting anybody off
    sitting too close, starting up conversation.
My company has arrived. Solitude herself.

— Gregory of Corkus

OLD FLAME

From Riverside Drive a cloud wraps the distant mountain in
   a mohair scarf, the type a woman drapes about her neck,
a female who jams words in my Adam's apple.
   The traffic is bottlenecked. The lights turn
from red to green and back to red. Too late.
   I notice my grey hair in the rearview mirror.
A woman strolls through my reflection. She is the image of one
   I vowed to spend my life with once. The traffic flows.
No going back now. Gone for ever, sipping takeaway coffee,
   her ambrosia this bitter morning. Old flame, old muse,
Mnemosyne's cold daughter, how faithfully cruel you are today.

— Gregory of Corkus

APPRECIATION

We treat the god of rain rather poorly, curse
    the drizzle, shower, downpour, hailstorm, torrent,
the cats and dogs, the deluge that cleared the air
    accompanied by Lightning and laggardly Thunder.
You'd think such insults would be too much for the god.
    Maybe at times they are and he throws a tantrum
and catches us without an umbrella at a football match
    or picnic, no shelter in sight. But this god is soft
by nature. Long may he reign. We forget that without him
    we'd be minus the multitudinous shades of green,
the harvests of Demeter, the gifts, bounty he showers
    on us. Bow down now before the god of precipitation,
this brooding god, the weeping god of the sky.

— Pluvius

180

WHITE OUT

The day gets away from me. Nothing done
　and it's lunchtime, rushing to a meeting,
held up by white-out traffic, the snow
　calling a halt to the daily life-and-death tedium:
committees, bills, email, post. If we croaked today
　what difference would it make? I give up,
tell myself to wait till the traffic eases off.
　Park. Drop into a shop. Watch the snow
erase the world. It is good to throw
　your hat at it all, not turn up, be nothing, no one,
watch the snow fall, turn to a blank page.

— Pluvius

GAIA'S INN

The owner informs us the inn's closed, summer's over,
    but we're welcome to a few beers, to sit on the deck.
We're sensible enough not to take any notice
    of the begging dog with the stick in his mouth.
Ignore him long enough and he'll give up
    just as the nagging mutt of weekday routine,
nitty-gritty responsibility, has left us be.
    Buoys tilt like planets, each with its own biosphere
of creatures and plants. Suds at the water's edge.
    It seems Gaia has washed her hands
of the motor-boat, the jet stream, the radio
    reporting the all-too-human news of the planet
heating up, that we, the only species which destroys
    its own habitat, is also the only one which creates gods.
The goddess reflects, "Ah, they've been deity-making for ever,
    making something of themselves, *Homo importanticus.*
Let's cut them slack. We'd be nothing without them.
    Let them be for now."

— Dogus

182

VISITING THE DELPHIC ORACLE

We climb to the oracle that people
    visit from distant islands with their supplications.
Temple Hocus-Pocus makes us feel better,
    conjures answers, gives us hope. Hope may be
the god who, down the ages, has been most
    necessary. Where would we be without hope?
We're so inventive, so hopelessly clever.

— Iono the Dramatist

PARADISE

To be inside on a wet day, rain on the roof,
    the heavens opening, the diamond drops draping
the window. Nothing to do but hunker in, snug
    under the quilt, in the armchair
by the fire with a book, or watch a game,
    no pressure to cut the grass, oil the bike,
clean the car, run to the bank, jog, swim —
    freed from the taskmaster of good weather.

— Dan the Younger

THE EVENT HORIZON

Perhaps those zones where our souls are said to end up
    are possible: that region the good inhabit, the one
where the imperfect are burnished perfect, the infernal place
    of no-hopers. The afterlife is no more unbelievable
than us landed here on this giant spinning-top
    whirling crookedly through space,

especially now the brains proclaim zones
    where time's altered, kaput; dimensions where stars slip
through self-generated cracks in space and so much more
    not dreamed of in our reality. Truly, after all, the soul
may have somewhere to go beyond the only event horizon
    we know of, our point of no return. Unbelievable.

— Mosius the Astronomer

THE LESSON

It's as though the god of unhappiness, of discontent at least,
    injected serum into our veins when born, inoculating us
from feeling good for long. He's like a grim schoolmaster
    patrolling the playground, reminding children
they have only a minute or two before the line-up bell,
    darkening unconscious happiness, marring natural mirth
with back-burner anxiety, fretful they'll have to line up soon
    and march back into interminable lessons, tests,
right and wrong answers, punishment, the classroom's gloom,
    learning by rote, the slow tick of the metronome,
the dolor of the adult world, that life isn't *all* play.

                                   — Patrikios

WISH YOU WERE HERE

As we drove through the countryside, dry
    as the donkey's back that a grizzled man rode
into the infinity of the mountains, nothing was
    so spectacular as the purple and white oleander
a local called *pikrodaphne*, nonchalant
    about that picture-postcard flower lining the roadway.
His eyes are dulled by what is
    under the purview of the god Familiarity. If only
we thought of ourselves as tourists visiting our planet,
    circling our heavenly star, writing postcards to ourselves
starting with: *Having a wonderful time. This place*
    is paradise, truly out of this world.

                                        — Longlius

TRAILER

Something about the quality of sea swaying in the bay at Hydra
     calls to mind the crowd in the Savoy Cinema long ago,
swaying in unison as everyone sang along with the organ-player,
     words rising line by line on the screen. We've forgotten
the name of the organ man, famous in our town
     at the earth's center. We've forgotten the lost world
of singalongs — singsongs we called them — gone the way
     of cold type, horse troughs, a particular texture of bread,
certain words. But right now everyone's swaying side
     to side, a great moving sea in an antique land.

                                        — Liamos of the South

TO A TEACHER
especially for Iono the Dramatist

Once more you stand before a cabal of *epheboi*,
instructing them how to look at the sun.
You pin-hole a sheet of paper.
The light is blacked out, then emerges
out of the night of the moon.
    Some pupils observe,
lit by learning, others show
not a glimmer of interest. How
can you guide them away
from eclipsing Acedia, Confusion,
Mammon: the dark gods of our day?
You bow your head as if before a shrine
reaching to set a candle alight.

— Terence of the North

TEENAGERS

They loiter, smoke, giggle, strut, cat whistle,
    shout obscenities, text, ogle
each other's crushes, torpedo into the Aegean.
    We hadn't heard school was out today,
curse these adultlets bursting with hormones,
    embarrassing to see as their acned faces,
their bodies sprouting hair. Don't be too
    hard on them. They're in
the cocoon agony, miserable, mortifying,
    alone. Ignoble to recall
even in old age. We should be kind,
    kindest of all to these. Spare them.

— Normanios the Physician

190

CHILDHOOD

You wax lyrical about childhood being idyllic,
    a country under a spell:
a beach ball in the air, an uncle with a trick
    of a penny up his sleeve, a lick
of ice cream, blithe waving from the horses of a carousel
    galloping the hills of childhood. Well,
okay, but look again while the impaled horses circle,
    their faces appear as if they're being whipped through hell.

— Honestmedon

EVENTUALLY

ton koimismenon

The pot of grief,
all that is left of you,
bubbling on the blue flower
of a slow flame,

left there evaporating,
slipping the mind,
the water
all
but boiled off.

— Honestmedon

A NEW LAW

Let there be a ban on every holiday.
    No ringing in the new year.
No fireworks doodling the warm night air.
    No holly on the door. I say
let there be no more.
    For many are not here who were here before.

— Honestmedon

PARENTS

What do any of us know about our parents,
    separate or together? My mother kept the house
in order, prepared food, wore the *epinetron* smooth
    rolling the threads, the skeins of daily love.
She wove our clothes, played knucklebones, snakes and ladders,
    lined up with other women at the well,
walked home balancing the vase on her head
    as she balanced our family, the *oikos*.
Like most parents she hid her care, the arguments
    with my father heading off on another odyssey.
Da played dead when I stabbed him, let me
    wear his helmet, turned into a tickle monster.
Ma scolded him for exciting me before bed.
    I suppose they were like most parents. What do I know?
I had no others. They were mysterious as the night sky, the god
    hidden within the dark of the forbidden inner temple.

Fragment from the lost poem *Telemachus*

— Danichorus

GODDESS OF THE HEARTH

And what about Hestia? We know little of her story.
　　Where's the record of Penelope
and Telemachus playing checkers before the fire?
　　Or the version in which Odysseus escaped the draft,
never left for Troy, enjoyed the solace
　　of arriving home after work, pouring a glass of wine,
romping with his boy, having given thanks to the goddess?
　　Hestia, as unassuming as so many wives, husbands,
parents slaving at chores without a word
　　of thanks, feeding the hearth, the embers rekindled.

— Heanius

CONCEALMENT

A man walked past. We practically
    brushed shoulders, the lane was so narrow.
I nodded, muttered a *kalimera*, but
    he chose to look ahead, ignore me.
I've seen that look, that demeanor before,
    always in rural towns, villages:
Toome, Morrisville, Derrynane, Delphi.
    Not simply the buttoned-up look that is the result
of living in a small community,
    but the face that stubbornly shuts out the invasion
of sightseers, yuppie realtors, outsiders.
    It conceals the gold bar of butter,
rancid or no, left buried in the bog,
    safe from any museum,
the last salted treasure of the lost world.

                                        — Heanius

THE GREEN LINE

Of all the roads, including the breathtaking cliff roads
    of Parnassus, the Healy Pass, or the drive over Coomakista,
the type of road we love most are those roadlings
    off the beaten track with grass breaking through
the tarred center, a green line: the one down to our house
    from the Pass of the Treasure, or the Serpentine Way,
a road where you might see a stoat, kingfisher, or badger.
    The grass is a sign, a grassroots' demonstration
led by Gaia, or Dana declaring "We shall overcome" or
    some such cliché. Daisies and dandelions shoot up
through asphalt, flowers stuck in the muzzles of guns.

                                     — Sirios

RESORT

The ocean wraps its surf scarf round the shoulder
of the shore. Everything's in touch with everything else:
    the sky with the sea, the wave susurrus
with the zephyr in the fuchsia and furze, the cock crowing
    again and again, dawning on us
every second is now. And then the invasion of day trippers
    — I among them, a scout,
already parked. The cars wind along the road
    glittering like the helmets of hoplites,
take over for a day; the legions
    of an empire going the way of all empires.

                                  — Antipater the Traveller

FOREIGNER

Good to be a stranger in a city, swan about
    its streets, lanes, quays, establish headquarters
in a café or tavern, get to know the regulars
    but not long enough to see their other sides,
or be taken for granted. You, the fresh slate, the tabula rasa.
    Everyone seems so amiable. The character who wears
his cap at a rakish angle, the geezer with his young wife,
    the chatty woman dressed in clothes too young for her.
Observe them tenderly: tipsy Pan, aging Aphrodite
    wearing a mini skirt, Zeus in from the rain,
his umbrella blown inside out, cursing "Boreas, that ass,"
    Leda giving you the eye — look out, trouble there.
Nothing like hobnobbing with the local pantheon.

— Antipater the Traveller

TEMPLENOE

The seine boats, colorful as jockeys, jockey each other
    at the starting line, named like racehorses:
El Niño, Rainbow Warrior, The Liberator, Challenge,
    Golden Feather, The Kingdom. With a shot they're off.
The crowd lets out yelps, incitements subduing even
    raffle sellers, ice cream van jingles, trinket stalls.
The holy gods of Tackiness are beaten for now by local gods
    inciting crews to win: the stocky helmsman of Waterville,
the shrewd one of Valentia, the determined one of Derrynane.
    The silver trophy glitters on Templenoe Pier, winks
that the gods of antiquity are with us still. Make no mistake
    about it. On Iveragh. Which one will lift the cup today?

— Liamos of the South

GOOD COMPANY

The water washes up around a rock like a wind-blown
    wedding veil, a child's hand in a passing car waves
to a waving whitethorn bush, the turquoise of shoreline sea
    and deeper teal far out are highlighted by the sun,
my smile reflects in your shades. Nothing exists
    without another. It's good not to be alone, be alive even,
better anyway than yesterday, that grey mist
    like a drear god descended and made nothing
of everything. Nothing. But forget that now. Yesterday
    is defined only via today and today thankfully
via yesterday: everything made out of nothing, rather
    than nothing made out of everything.

— Connectinus

SERMON

. . . we have a saviour who has been tempted in every way, just as we are — yet without sin

Hebrews 4:15

These days the Savior could not come back
to live without sin among us, the matrix beneath the surface
    of daily existence being sewn so intricately
by that crafty dark angel, tireless Complicity.
    God's temples are heated by oil secured at the expense
of slaughter. The pillows He'd lie on are the down
    of the bird that saved Noah. Even sackcloth
would likely have molecules of blood in its stitches.
    He can't simply drop down, mosey
around town, take in His handiwork: trees rising up
    from concrete, the hubbub of folk about their chores,
a passing woman who reminds Him of Magdalene, the smell
    of coffee. How He envies the creature
created in His own image. How He longs to become His image.
    How He pines for this earth. How absurd
the old God feels now. Our Image. Pray for Him.

— Simeon the Second

ON THE MAKE

Sunday morning, the train emerges not just from the tunnel
    of Penn Station, across from the Catacombs,
the Palisades, the shining lordly Hudson, but from the hell
    of another excursion to hustle for my poems.
Enough. Head north to my hermitage.
    Know again the rapture of the pen across the page.

— John the Maker

DROPPING NAMES

To go unnoticed is good, though mostly we forget
    and silently crave attention, fame,
to be seen, adored even, above all others — unseemly.
    Listen to rain's patter on your hut
away from everyone. If you have any need to drop a name
    then hobnob with the likes of demigod Solitude
or the irenic deity of the rain, an unseen local god
    whose name's long forgotten, or still unknown.

— Arion

UNDERSTORY

Redwood sorrel adapts so well to light levels
    that its heart-shaped leaf
folds down and hides under direct sunshine,
    opens up in shade, diffused rays. We're not
unlike that plant, never getting far from earth,
    hardly able to take the fierce light of joy,
or bliss, nor the pitch night
    of despair or fear. We survive best
in the shadows, the understory of our days.

    — Thomas the Gardener

TO ANOTHER DAILY GOD

Today I want to thank the daily god of unhappiness,
   petty worries, disgruntlements, sorrows great
and small, for having taken such good care of me,
   making himself at home in my days,
and for taking the odd break as now he slips away
   into the background, smiling kindly perhaps,
giving me over to his reclusive sibling, Peace,
   at a traffic light on Pearl and Union. The sun
softens the snow-bordered street, the ice-cased lake.
   We turn into our clearer selves like snow and rime
turn to water. I wave a driver ahead. He avidly
   waves thanks. I would like to wave
gratitude to the god of unhappiness.
   He could've finished me off often enough.
His present absence highlights my happytime.

— Antonel of Carrucius

THE MOST NEGLECTED GOD OF ALL

Now let us praise the most neglected god of all,
   the god of the Hand Job, Hand Shandy, Master
Spank the Monkey, Madame Frig. The god
   that everyone: housewives, presidents, gurus,
Zen monks — so that's the One Hand Clap — rabbis, nuns
   are possessed by, ever since it was handed down
to Pan who in turn handed it on to shepherds. The god Atum,
   who the Egyptians say gave rise to us all —
not the Big Bang then, but The Big Hand Job. The god
   pouts that we never pay him public due.
We're ashamed, embarrassed at having lit
   a furtive candle to him. Myriads down
through the ages have attended his daily secret service
   wherever the members of his church could find:
offices, buses, alleys, bathrooms, beaches, cars.
   There's hardly a spot on earth
people haven't laid their offering. What's the strangest place
   you've communed with this handy god? Even as we speak,
millions of hands are busy all over the world.
   You yourself may have been blessed by him today.
Have you given thanks? Enough of turning a blind eye,
   of being small, stunted. Come now.

— Panus

THE LADYKILLER

Suddenly, catching myself in the mirror,
    — hard to figure what precipitated this shift,
appropriately in The Old Town Bar — the timeless self-image
    of a curly, handsome twenty-something-year-old
fell away before my eyes and I saw this unfamiliar
    grey-haired chap, hair receding above his temple.
Only this morning the world was at my feet, God's gift
    to women, a ladykiller. The Graiae, three crones
born white-haired, nudge each other on nearby stools.
    My new girlfriends flirt with me, only one tooth
between them in their snickering heads.

— Gregory of Corkus

THE GOAT

When you reach to help the hurt creature,
    it usually reacts in fear
— what does it know of goodwill? Remember
    that day on Coomakista Pass
the goat that had trapped its head
    in a wire box fence. No matter
from what angle we patiently approached,
    it bucked,
the wire cutting into its neck all the more
    till finally we gave up. The memory
of that goat returns, I
    being in the grip of old ways,
old goat ways I never
    seem to slip free of, helpless
to untangle goathead, desperate
    to hold to that one security.
At least this he knows. At least this
    is certain.

                                        — Rakius

A QUIET GLORY
to Antonel of Carrucius and Davus the Consul

You must hold on after all these years
   of natter about sport, pulchritude, the state
of the world. The repetition of wilting stories.
   When all else fails — Eros, family, work —
it has been faithful, supportive on bad days
   like the trellis set in the earth so that hardy climbers,
glories, can wind their way up. Without friendship,
   maybe the greatest of all glories, you'll not fully bloom.

— Vermontus

LAUGHTER

On Center Street, Skala, fuming with traffic,
   tired-faced mothers wheel prams, processions
of schoolchildren wave flags,
   commemorating another military victory
— Ares smiling smugly on his infants.
   Three old women chat outside
the laundromat. I haven't a clue about what
   they say, but it's mirthful. The woman
without spectacles breaks
   into laughter, bends over in stitches
with a heartiness I haven't witnessed for ages
   at whatever the others say.
They've taken everything from life, wear black
   for all the reasons women wear black.
They've outshone even their own God,
   the orthodox God who never laughed.
May the memory of these women, the three graces,
   be with me now and in the hours of our blackness.

— Davus the Consul

THE OTHER

Time to raise a paean to the olive-green slugs, mauve
maggots, slime-emerald algae, dandruff-creamy worms
who make nothing of the corpse. The diverse bugs
we turn our heads away from, loathsome swarms,
steaming dung dolloped on soil that springs roses,
thyme, tomatoes, the food on our tables. Doff our hats
to all matter and mites we look down our snotty noses
on. Admit that we are myopic, dumb, stupid, bats
— praise the bats too — that we're the great ungrateful.
Say thanks, erect monuments to them, the other beautiful.

— Panos Kinnellus

THE WINNER

The bluebottle reigns supreme now
    over the kingdom of a carcass —
it doesn't matter to the fly if it's a cow,
    rat, salmon, human, or ass.
The bluebottle is a glimmering gem
    not on Death's, but on Life's diadem.

— Panos Kinnellus

WONDER OF WONDERS

A girl cries. Her father beats her, convinces her she's dumb.
    She'll land back in that cave of herself again and
again for the rest of her life. Many are like mythical characters
    blindly returning to tackle whatever invisible monsters
brought them down long ago. Maybe the wonder
    of wonders of being alive — greater even than the lake
like a glittering shield, the leaves turning tangerine,
    bronze, ruby and so infinitely on — is, as yet,
we have not completely undone our world.
    And should we each manage to wrestle
our own particular Trauma to the ground and tame him,
    there is Thanatos — his natural father — waiting
at the end of it all, the Bigwig behind all the trouble.
    Time to give ourselves a pat on the back, breathe
a sigh, for not having blown ourselves sky high.

— Bernardius Scholasticus

THE TRAVELLER'S GRACE

Nothing like landing in a foreign city
    early morning. Preferably in weekday hubbub.
Everyone going about their business, lost in themselves,
    not a thought of how strange, foreign, alien their lives are.
How abnormal to think it normal to find ourselves
    on a spinning ball reeling around a star
at thousands of miles per hour from who knows where
    to who knows where. How outlandish.
I'm one of the sacred dead,
    released from the underworld
of the mundane, the banal. Behold the normal.

— Gregoris Plenipanómenos

Translations of Contemporary Irish Language Poets

SEAHORSE

The seahorse is not a great swimmer.
He grasps sea vegetation
with his long tail
but the currents
sweep him away.
He's carried beyond his ken.

Oceanic passion.
I don't have a grip on any secure thing,
a seahorse
on a foamy voyage.
Is this what's called
eternity?
If so, it can go to the devil.
I'll be flotsam washed up on a stony beach
I will be desiccated
and set among Curios
in a Heritage Centre.
You'll come to gawk at me
(or your children, maybe);
my name in English, Latin and Irish:
Seahorse/Hippocampus/Capall Mara.
You'll not know me.
You will pass on
to the next glass case,
your shoes a hollow
echo on the floor.

Translated from Gabriel Rosenstock

SONG

On your journey far from home I think of you.
Christmas separated us, then passed away.
The eddying wind that flung us together
wouldn't shake a chestnut from a branch now.

Though we may never meet again,
do not think that you have been forgotten.
Remember me on your walks from time to time
on Inisbofin or wherever you find yourself.

The longing in your eyes still moves me
and your breasts still surge on my chest.
Our body heat outwitted that Jack Frost night.
In the morning two porcelain swans drifted on the lake.

We headed off together through country,
creating space for our secrets. They are now
in the possession of Ireland's mountains and valleys
while we fall apart on a single telephone line.

Translated from Liam Ó Muirthile

WHAT IT IS

I go from room to room
around the house
looking for something,
and, to be honest, I won't know
what it is
till I find it.

It's not the bread tin,
nor the coarse brown flour,
nor the fine white flour,
though I take them out
and measure them on the scales
and bake a single loaf.

It's not any book I was devouring,
if memory serves me correctly,
which I put down absent-mindedly,
although I stand at the shelves
and scan the book stacks
and fall to my knees.

It's not any missing key.
I wasn't going out.
I didn't leave anything on, although
I'm shuffling from room to room,
combing the whole house for something
and it's nothing
quietly mourning.

Translated from Liam Ó Muirthile

Uncollected Poems

THE SOCK MYSTERY

There should be an asylum for single socks,
lost, dejected, turned in on themselves.
The twin sock, soul mate, doppleganger gone AWOL,
on the lam, slipping through a time-space warp
somewhere within the module of the washing machine
or dryer rattling in the cellar's deep space.
The one never to be found again. Gone
we know not where, to the afterlife of socks,
Sock Tartarus; the Elysium of Argyle; the heaven
of crew, gold toe, tennis, winter wooly, summer wear.
Surely there's no purgatory or hell for socks,
even for absconders who walk out on partners, family,
before their soles are worn threadbare, their number up.
The odd time it happens these socks get lonely
for the earth, and weeks, months later the prodigals
meekly reappear under a bed, cushion, wardrobe, only
to discover their partners have disappeared,
passed on, unable to make it alone. But how good
it is to see socks united once more, tucked
into each other, close, touching, at one,
the deserter promising to stay put, not to take a hike,
not do a runner this time. No greater joy is known
than on these occasions, such dancing, such cavorting,
such jubilation in the kingdom of socks.

TO MY MOTHER
(Marymount Hospice, Cork)

Tonight I keep watch over you dying,
the most peaceful night I ever knew.
I suppose it's the release of your going
drawn out over chemo months into

years. I soothe your agitated hand. You lie
under the nightlight's nimbus, reflected within
the black window — your bed and you fly
in the pane above the city's Saturday-night din.

Pure Chagall. You head into the stars,
over Summerhill, Capwell, Evergreen, the Black Ash;
hover above familiar streets and lanes, bars
folk sing in. There is no need to dash.

Your name has just been noble-called.
Sing "South of the Border" one last time. You
raise your voice above the Lee, the town you hauled
a lifetime of plastic bags through,

bowing into the drizzle, drudging home
along North Main Street, up Blarney Lane;
our city of hills, our Frisco, our Rome,
our Buenos Aires, our Varanasi. Rain weeps on the pane.

Your hand must be waving adios. Ma,
the night sky reflects our city below.
Now every light's a votive candle, your Fatima.
Behold the glass darkly. There you go.

ELEGY

to a friend with Alzheimer's

Your memory was dispatched ahead
   of you to the land of Orcus
— the spool of all you are, to yourself, erased
    though not to us.
This is as good as addressing the dead.
Your body's a blood hound baying, the scent lost
   at that last river. Dumb, but tell Mnemosyne,
    or the boss of Lethe,
or whatever god's your final host,
    that my heart's a clenched fist.
You are a man alive dearly missed.

TO THOSE WHO STAYED

Brand us *exiles*, *emigrants* if you like.
It may make your life easier, may buttress
you, shield you, maybe even help hike
your spirits up, help you feel superior to us.

You will need it as you traverse streets
that you brag you can walk blindfold on.
But where's that shop, that bar? No one greets
you any more; so many are dead, or, like us, gone.

Perhaps we were shrewder, wiser, more cunning.
Perhaps not. What's certain is that more
and more your town is abandoning you, forgetting
you, as if the town itself is crossing to another shore,

leaving you nothing and no one, an immigrant
in your own place, the oblivious emigrant.

BLUES

There's a brilliant, but intangible lazulite blue
— you must have seen it — glistening off fresh snow,
something akin, but not quite the same as you
see shine off the back of a barn swallow,
the star-and-moon bling-ed night sky,
the neck of the male mallard, the halo
of a gas-stove flame, a certain neon butterfly,
or the back of a bluebottle fly. This ineffable glow
I noticed again seeing students, both unwhite,
Manny and Ty Prince, shimmering blue light
as they high-fived by the International Garden
outside my office. I didn't cotton on till then
why in the Irish language a black brother and sister
are called blue. O, my beautiful blue sister and brother.

UMBILICAL

You bike most everywhere these days,
wary of your part in the latest war, the slaughter
of innocents, the various wily ways

you've grown used to, complicity's tether.
The gas pump is an umbilical cord
sucking the life out of exhausted Terra Mater.

You read about leaders ready to award
the future and Mammon her body, smother
her in her own fumes. You know the reward,

the fate of those who kill their mothers.
Remember *Orestes* you translated to *Humankind*.
Down swoop the Erinyes, the avenging daughters,

driving tormented Orestes out of his mind.
No escaping the Furies now, the ever so kind.

CANTICLE OF THE SUN

(A secular take, with apologies to Francis of Assisi)

Chalk it down. Never so much as now should we praise
    the maker. First, let us praise Brother Sun. He
is the light that alights out of every night. He is
    the radiant first offspring of the One.
Next let us praise Sister Moon, and all the stars like manna
    showering down from the heavens.
Let us praise Weather himself: the twins Air and Wind,
    Cloud and Sky who sustain all creatures.
What about their sibling, Water? She is so humble
    she's hardly noticed. We'd be nothing without her.
Likewise our friend, Fire. And laud Mother Earth,
    carrying her basket overflowing
with sundry victuals to feed all her offspring:
    the ant, cow, rat, bee, vulture, bird
of paradise, crow, whale, camel, rainbow trout; all
    our close relatives. Applaud also those who work
for her sake, especially now we need them more
    than ever. They know we have
so little time, that we've made our mother ill.
    Praise those who say there is hope still, and those
who struggle for peace peacefully. They'll be crowned
    in the maker's goodness before the end,
which is always now and without end. We could go on,
    but let us finish by praising Father Death, for he is
of the creator. Those who do not honor him bring him on us
    before our time. Yet those who struggle for our mother
know another life. May they thrive. Yea, I say, chalk it down.

S

With the snaky handle of simply one letter the word,
unsheathed from its own scabbard, becomes sword.

THE HELLBOXER

The nine bitches have put a match to him.
"We're suckin' diesel now, folks. Look out,"
he cries, recasting himself daily in flame.
Here cometh the *great* work, no doubt,
and he doubts everything — including
doubt. Who cares, especially himself,
as long as the words come, pouring
molten from him, harden into books on a shelf?
What a conflagration. "This is thirsty work.
A drink please." No better man to suckle the milk
of Mother Stereotype. Pop goes another cork.
Who's he chatting up now? Typical of his ilk.
The re-newer of the Word, a dismal paradox.
His type cast in the flames of his very own hellbox.

And he thought, way back, he could pull it off
and remain unbroken, unburnt, much to muse ire.
He didn't hear the nine pyrotechnists laugh:
"Time to turn up the heat, make a human bonfire
of this devil. Show him who's who. What attitude."
Mind you, they warmed to him when he told
his tearful mother — flaring into a family feud —
he'd be a poet, a corker one at that. Sixteen years old
and none too bright. She begged him on her knees to
consider bank teller, office clerk, any sensible job.
"How'll you make a living? All we've done for you."
His da looked out of sorts. Flames shot from her gob.
"Besides, you can always write poems in your leisure."
She was just a middleclass dragon minding her treasure.

He swore to himself that before it was all over,
he'd call a halt, put his pencil away,
hang up the cork gun, quietly duck for cover,
dodge muse abuse. Even the Big G took a day
off. More than thrice he's heard the cock crow.
Time to reverse, take up the vocation that
as a boy he prayed to have: "When I grow
up, I'd like to be a saint, Lord." He played at
being humble, pulled off a miracle or two,
blessed the wicked and poor, renounced desire,
did penance for the world. Christ, it came true
perversely, as he hellboxed in the daily pyre

of being saint and sinner in one. The fire still whips.
He is Jesus planting the betraying kiss on Judas' lips.

Index of Titles

Index of First Lines